Gardening in your Nightie

What every passionate gardener should know, but never dared to ask ...

Helen Yemm

EBURY PRESS
LONDON

This book is dedicated to my mother, Marie Yemm,
my original Nightie Gardener

*I would like to thank Lisa Pendreigh of Ebury Press, who is definitely getting
the hang of it all, and Barbara Levy, my agent, as well as my former students
who provided the inspiration for this book. I am also grateful to Susan Berry,
the green-fingered Veronica Hanson, Richard Zatloukal, and my friends at
Merriments Gardens for their invaulable twopennyworths. Last but not least,
I am indebted to my family, in particular to Chris, for unfailing moral support
and encouragement and the late Mr. Grumpy, who also helped.*

First published in the United Kingdom in 2000

3 5 7 9 10 8 6 4 2

Text © Helen Yemm, 2000
Photographs © Ebury Press, 2000

Helen Yemm has asserted her right to be identified as the author of this
work under the Copyright, Designs and Patents Act, 1988.

First published in the United Kingdom in 2000 by Ebury Press
Random House · 20 Vauxhall Bridge Road · London SW1V 2SA

Random House Australia (Pty) Limited
20 Alfred Street · Milsons Point · Sydney · New South Wales 2061 · Australia

Random House New Zealand Limited
18 Poland Road · Glenfield · Auckland 10 · New Zealand

Random House South Africa (Pty) Limited
Endulini · 5a Jubilee Road · Parktown 2193 · South Africa

Random House Group Limited Reg. No. 954009

A CIP catalogue record for this book is available from the British Library

ISBN: 0 09 187071 2

Designed by Lovelock & Co.
Photographs by Ben Rigby
Edited by Susan Berry

Printed and bound by Butler and Tanner Ltd, Frome, Somerset.

Gardening in your nightie

Contents

introduction

Some years ago, during a lull in the cut-and-thrust, question-and-answer part of one of my gardening classes, some bright spark, no doubt jolted from a domestic reverie and feeling the need to show keenness by volunteering a question, asked 'What do you wear when you are gardening?' I always tell my nervous novices that, on my gardening course, no question is too daft, so I answered this one in all seriousness.

As everyone who has ever 'caught' gardening, this disease of middle age, will testify, you *garden in your nightie*. And wet slippers. However, now that I have joined the frozen band of country gardeners, I would amend this answer: in fact, pyjamas are more practical because you can roll the legs up when trailing through the long grass to the garden heap with a lump of tree that has fallen in the night. And, when it is really frosty, you sometimes have the foresight to grab a fleece jacket, usually the nearest one to hand, inevitably 'XL' and filthy, as you 'just pop out for a second' into your own personal land of the lotus-eaters: the garden.

My answer seemed to strike a chord in the hearts of most of those still awake in the room. For thus it is the length and breadth of Britain. In the early hours of the morning, women – for it is they who do most of the graft these days – trail around their gardens, with a long-gone-cold cup of instant clutched in hand, as they plan, plot and dream, interrupting their reverie to tweak here, poke there, or, occasionally, hitching up their nightwear, plunge into the back of a border to nip off an errant shoot, perhaps.

Advanced symptoms of the condition manifest themselves in various ways. To find out if you have fallen prey, ask yourself the following questions. Have you ever tried to cut wire with kitchen scissors already blunted by trimming the edge of the lawn? Or teetered on a wonky kitchen stool, flailing around uncertainly with rusty loppers in a cloud of sagging honeysuckle in a force nine gale at 6am? And succeeded in pruning the washing line?

Perhaps, like me, you have stopped yourself in the nick of time from trying to open a bag of bonemeal with your teeth. If these sound familiar to you, then you, too, have succumbed.

For the lucky few, these shenanigans do not stop; they can go on for the best part of the morning, punctuated, perhaps, by a dash to the house to grab a piece of kitchen paper to wipe a drip from a frozen nose when cuffs become too soily to do the job efficiently, to be cut short only by the arrival of a bemused visitor at the front door. For an increasing number, however, these early morning raids, shortly after dawn, are the principal gardening time in the week. A glance at a mucky watch, however, has them scurrying indoors, scrubbing the soil from their knees and fingernails, throwing on their power clothes and rushing to work, leaving the sartorial secrets of their muddy habit strewn damply over the unmade bed. Take it from one who knows…

So this modest gardening book is for all you kindred souls, fellow sufferers of the gardening bug. It is for those of you who have been scratching about lovingly but less than effectively in your gardens in inappropriate clothes, with equally inappropriate tools, with sodden hair and a wrecked back, wondering all the while whether you have been doing more harm than good. It is for those of you who hate using gardening gloves 'because you can't feel things properly', and for whom the idea of 'a good night in' is a bottle of cheap red and a new fantasy-feeding book full of pictures of the misty-moisty gardens of the rich and organized. It is for those of you for whom there is never enough time or money, but who know deep down in your aching bones that gardening could be the ultimate pleasure if only you knew just a little bit more about it. This book is intended to give you, as one of my students succinctly put it, just enough to get you going, but not enough to scare you stiff.

There are, as you will have noticed on your first perfunctory flip through of this book, no glamorous photos to distract you into idle day-dreaming or irrational shopping trips, no tedious step-by-step instructions from a model with immaculate fingernails on how to make up a lurid hanging basket, and no quick'n'easy instant gardening DIY projects from a grinning TV garden designer. What follows is simple information and advice based on my own experience as a passionate gardener that will, I hope, make your time spent gardening easier and more rewarding.

CHAPTER 1

What a Lot of Gardeners Don't Know and Don't Like to Ask

As I write, there are scores of perfectly competent gardeners scratching away in their beloved oases as happy as sand boys but for that occasional, irritating thought that there is a whole lot of stuff about plants that they just don't know, and that had they done so it might have made their horticultural lives a little easier. I am not talking about advanced botany, or serious science, but the basic things that are so often taken for granted that we know – the lack of real understanding of which can eat away at our self confidence as gardeners and consequently get in the way of imaginative gardening. It is all a bit like those early school experiences that dog you for the rest of your life. I think I was 'away' the first time my class encountered long division. I never ever got the hang of it, and I have never ever dared ask anyone to explain it to me since. My subsequent terror of maths, I am convinced, stems from that time. Thank God for calculators.

If you walk round a garden with its really learned owners, they will explain everything and anything to you, for most love to talk. But you are hardly likely to stop them in mid-flow to ask them what they mean when they say such-and-such is a useful biennial. More probably you won't get to ask the really meaty questions that are burning within for fear of revealing scores of gaps in your basic knowledge and looking silly. Furthermore, gardeners are hopelessly generous and in return for your appreciation, will invariably press trowelsful of their treasures or, even worse, branches of rare shrubs for you to 'take a few cuttings' from, all of them with incomprehensible Latin names. It is all supposed to be part of the fun, a tangible expression of the overwhelming need of most gardeners to share their enthusiasm with others.

And what about all that Latin, which more than anything seems to fill people with horror? The fact that we no longer study Latin in most of our schools seems a huge shame. Initially I hated the subject as much as most, but began to realize fairly early on that Latin not only held the key to English spelling but also helped to lessen one's fear of learning other European languages. After an otherwise hopelessly flawed school career – I think I could best be described as detention-seeking – my Latin has become a welcome reminder that I am not without a brain. All those jars of broad beans that mouldered away on the school lab windowsill when everyone else's flourished, all that stuff about amoeba and spirogyra, the life-cycle of the tapeworm, and questions on the natural vegetation of the Tundra – freesias, was my oh-so-bright response, I recall – went in one ear and out of the other. But my comfort with Latin has really helped. Thank you Miss Prentice, wherever you are, with your Dame Edna specs and passion for all things Roman.

It was not till I started gardening, however, that I really discovered the value of Latin. The binomial system of naming plants, as it is called, dates back to the eighteenth century, when a Swedish botanist, Carl Linnaeus, decided that all plants should be given Latinized names (actually many of the generic names come from Greek) consisting of two words: the name of the **genus**, (e.g. *Potentilla, Skimmia, Delphinium* or whatever) and the name of the **species** (e.g. *fruticosa, nepalensis, japonica, alba, neumanniana*, or some such). Thus the 'surname' comes first, and the 'first name' comes second. Heaven only knows what kind of chap Linnaeus was, and can you imagine what kind of gardener he must have been? I bet poor old Mrs. Linnaeus (Linnaeus mrs. kitchenensis, perhaps?) had a hard job stopping him planting things in rows and putting labels on everything.

The reason why we are stuck with an embellished form of this ancient system is because it really is necessary. We simply cannot get by with common 'English' names because they don't describe the plant as accurately. I use common names whenever I can do so without causing confusion: how can we just abandon such evocative gems as lady's mantle, love-in-the-mist, granny's bonnet, love-lies-bleeding, Solomon's seal, lily-of-the-valley and so many more? So, like many, I use a confusing jumble of names, a compromise, in rather the same way that I have managed partially to convert to metric measurements: I am more than capable of saying that such-and-such is three feet high and thirty centimeters wide, and most people don't bat an eyelid. But we do need to take it all on board. I will therefore try to give a broad outline of how the system works as simply as I can, while apologising to real botanists (including my bemused mother) for probably over-simplifying the whole issue.

I shall use the following plants to illustrate my description: *Potentilla fruticosa arbuscula*, *Potentilla fruticosa* 'Elizabeth' and *Potentilla nepalensis* 'Miss Willmott'. I have chosen *Potentilla* as an example since I am asked from time to time by peeved students why it is that the sad little sprawly *Potentilla* they put in their own garden bears so little resemblance to the familiar shrubby pale yellow one resplendent all summer long in their parent's/friend's garden.

All plants belong in 'families', the members of which share certain botanical characteristics which may or may not be obvious to gardeners. If you look closely at the individual flowers of sweetpeas, laburnum and clover, for example, you will see they are very similar. They all belong to the pea family (*LEGUMINACEAE*). If you visit a botanic garden, you will find plants grown in large beds with other members of their family. It is quite a good way of putting the jigsaw puzzle together, but actually the family names of plants are, I think, the least important part of a plant's name, from our point of view. The **genus** *Potentilla* belongs, incidentally, to the rose family (*ROSACEAE*). The genus contains both **shrubs** and **herbaceous perennials** (see below). This is why the name *Potentilla* (or cinquefoil, a corruption of French, which is the 'English' name) on its own is pretty unhelpful, particularly when you are out shopping.

The vital second word on a plant label, or in a reference book, is the **species** name and will often, but by no means always, tell you a lot about the plant. It will describe either how it looks or smells, tell you where it comes from or even tell you the name of the person who first found it growing in the wild and brought it into cultivation. This is generally the part of the plant name that gives new gardeners the collywobbles, but it is not too hard to learn a few of the more obvious ones which are related to English words, and find a book that tells you the meaning of the more obscure-sounding ones. *Potentilla fruticosa* is a shrubby or woody (which is what '*fruticosa*' means) plant, *Potentilla nepalensis* (from Nepal) happens to be a herbaceous or non-woody one. Even if you do not have the energy to get to grips with the actual meaning of each one, you really need to know that this part of the name is important.

I am afraid there is more, much more. There is generally a third word (sometimes Latinized, sometimes English) on the plant label. This is the **variety** name – a further category which helps to identify plants more precisely. If it is a naturally occurring variation in a plant, say a different leaf or flower colouration, then it will be quite simple – *variegata* (variegated), *alba* (white), *hirsutum* (hairy) and so on. Hence *Potentilla fruticosa arbuscula* (meaning something like 'shrubby little bush'). If it is a cultivated variety, now often shortened to 'cultivar' (i.e. one that has occurred since it became a garden plant) then it will often have a recognizable English or other European language name written within quotes. Thus *Potentilla fruticosa* 'Elizabeth', or *Potentilla nepalensis* 'Miss Willmott'.

So, returning to the query from the peeved student. What she most likely did was to go for the word '*Potentilla*' on the garden centre label. What she probably wanted was *Potentilla fruticosa* 'Abbotswood', or 'Elizabeth', but acquired by mistake *Potentilla nepalensis* 'Miss Willmott' or 'Gibson's Scarlet' (popular **cultivars** of a **herbaceous species** of the same **genus** – got that?) by mistake.

And then there are **hybrids**, which occur when two species from the same genera are deliberately crossed. If you see multiplication signs in the middle of plant names, this indicates a hybrid, for example, *Primula x bulleesiana* is a hybrid between *Primula beesiana* and *Primula bulleyana*… This is the point at which most of us glaze over and switch on the telly for light relief, so I will draw a veil over the rest. Suffice it to say that **F1 hybrids** are hybrids with attitude – plants with greater vigour, better flowers and often greater disease resistance. More than that the average gardener really, really does not need to know.

While on the subject of hybrids, I have a few pet hates. The introduction of so many new garden plant varieties and hybrids is, in my view, a sign that horticulture has gone mad. I suppose I can understand the reason for breeding plants to promote improved disease resistance, more intense scent and, perhaps, even bigger and better flowers, all of which matter to a lot of gardeners. However, I am sure I am not alone in looking sideways at some of those awful recent additions – such as 'Jolly Joker' pansies, and the variegated *Spirea, Ceanothus* and *Cistus* which I think look either sick or totally alien or both.

Another pet hate is the way botanists periodically get into huddles and change plant names, usually when they think we gardeners are getting a bit too cocky. How many young(ish) gardeners have parents who still insist on calling *Philadelphus* (commonly known as mock orange), '*Syringa*', when everyone under the age of 50 knows *Syringa* is now the Latin name for lilac? And did you know that ubiquitous evergrey shrub with those love 'em or hate 'em yellow ragwort flowers is no longer called '*Senecio*', but is now *Brachyglottis*? I suppose we should be grateful as we never could make up our minds whether to pronounce it SeNEKio or SenEESio. But the new name sounds like a nasty throat infection however you say it. And that lovely weeping bamboo *Arundianaria murieliae* is now apparently called *Fargesia murieliae*, although rumour has it that it has been changed yet again Maybe that is why all the wonderful specimens that were around ten years ago flowered with a vengeance, wept their last and died. Trying to keep up with it all makes me feel very weary, it really does.

Which brings me to pronunciation. Many obsessed gardeners spend a lot of time thumbing through books and mumbling darkly to themselves without a clue as to how the real world works. If you care that much about 'accepted' pronunciation, you can get one of those books on plant names that will give you their phonetic pronunciation. If you don't, then just keep your ears open and you will be amazed at what you hear coming out of the mouths of even 'those who should know'. Once when I was appearing on the same television programme as Peter Seabrook (he of the elegant shock of white hair, lugubrious smiley voice and a certain way with leeks and potatoes), we each pronounced the name *Lysimachia punctata* totally differently, bold as brass, for all to hear. And guess what? The world did not come to an end.

Incidentally, I have noticed that whenever a few friendly gardeners get together they invariably have a good laugh about mutual mispronunciations. The name *Cotoneaster* springs to mind. I think most of us have been members of the Cotton Easter club. As I say, who cares?

Returning briefly and absolutely finally to the subject of the necessity for Latin names, there is now a more pressing reason to persevere with them. If you happen, as I do, to start 'oohing' and 'aahing' about plants in garden centres in foreign parts, you can 'ooh' and 'aah' together with foreign gardeners *in Latin*. (I just love to hear Italians speak Latin. I suspect that even their words for horse manure sound like the finer parts of a Catholic Mass.) Latin names do make you feel very grown up. And while I have yet to find something as simple as a bag of bonemeal in a French garden centre I find that buying plants there is, comparatively speaking, a doddle.

I should hate this book to become one of those useful but dry little numbers – an A to Z of largely obscure horticultural terms. You sense that the writer of such books has been dredging around trying to fill each letter section with as many definitions as he or she can find to make you realize how much there is you don't know about plants and gardening. I will try to include explanations of key words within each section of the book, but I do think it is important to understand exactly what the following means before you read on.

An **annual** plant is one that completes its growing cycle during one season and will not survive frost. This group of plants includes petunias, busy Lizzies, nasturtiums and so on, and most of them need a lot of sun. The term **hardy annual** applies to those plants whose seeds can be sown directly into the ground in spring or even autumn. Their seeds germinate as soon as the soil is warm enough and the days long enough – they then cope with whatever Mother Nature throws at them. Many hardy annuals will therefore self-seed, so that once you introduce plants such as love-in-the-mist, marigolds or nasturtiums into your garden, you will find that they become a more or less a permanent fixture, which is quite fun. Most annuals, however, are tender and have to be raised from seed in a warm greenhouse or on a windowsill indoors. Being expensive to buy and time-consuming to maintain, they should be grown in pots and other containers, used to create bright spots of colour or fill gaps in a new garden. My real favourites are the big annuals: cosmos, cleome and tobacco plants. You have to make sure you get hold of *Nicotiana affinis* if you want those big, white tobacco plants that glow in the dark and knock you sideways with their scent. (I have actually known garden centre staff to fib about what they offer you. Many of the modern cultivars available are miserable little scentless things, I find). These larger annuals, real floppy whoppers, spend the midsummer months achieving their often breath-taking height, and then reward you with flowers well into the early autumn, when the rest of the average British garden can look a bit sad and burnt out. At the end of autumn, pull out any annuals and chuck them away, even though they may look as though they want to jolly on past Christmas.

A **biennial** plant is one that takes two growing seasons to complete its cycle. During the first year the new seedlings produce a small amount of rather uninteresting leaf growth but do not flower. If they survive the ravages of slugs, snails and fanatical weeders until the next year, they will produce loads of flowers, millions of seeds and die a very ugly and dramatic death at the end of the summer. The most well-known examples are foxgloves, honesty and forget-me-nots. It is really important to identify biennials when they are very young – you can do this by comparing the leaves of the baby and the adult – because you can quite easily transplant biennials after their first year of growth. Indeed it is generally necessary to thin the seedlings out where they make colonies and threaten to stunt each other's growth. I adore the self-seeding biennial population of my garden – constantly ebbing and flowing, providing bits of haphazard colour in unexpected places. If it threatens to overwhelm, I just weed it.

There is a variation to biennials. Some plants, notably angelica and some verbascums, are what is known as **monocarpic**, which means they may take more than two years to become mature enough to flower and set seed, after which they generally die.

A **perennial** (also referred to as a **herbaceous perennial**) is a frost-hardy, non-woody plant (in other words not a shrub) which comes up year after year. In this group are the favourite summer flowerers – lupins, delphiniums, campanulas and so on. As I explain in the chapter on mixed borders (see pages 80–85), perennials do need a certain amount of attention – protection from slugs, annual feeding, supporting with canes or twigs, dead-heading to keep them flowering for as long as possible, cutting down to ground level in the winter and division every few years – but they are incredibly rewarding once established. A few, generally short-lived perennials (such as the Welsh poppy and sweet rocket) will seed themselves gently around the garden. I love that, and it is one of the main reasons it is so important to learn to distinguish seedlings from weedlings.

In small gardens which, it has to be acknowledged, most of us start off with, **annuals** and **biennials** are best planted in groups of at least three in order to make a decent statement, while **perennials** (which should eventually form extremely large clumps), should be planted singly or quite close together in pairs, which can be separated a year or so later. I am well aware the accepted 'rule' is that you should always plant in odd numbers, but what you do depends on the size of the plants in question, and the amount of space available. It always pays to do a bit of homework before you acquire plants you are not sure about. A friend, a true horticultural innocent clearly under the influence of someone with a garden far larger than her own 50ft by 30ft patch, once bought *three* young plants of *Crambe cordifolia* (ultimately vast, really vast, perennials). She planted them 2ft apart in the middle of a border no more than 10ft long and 4ft wide, together with other plants, none of them small. Fortunately the *Crambe* all died. If you are lucky enough to have loads of space, you can plant perennials in great interlocking swaths, known to posh gardeners as 'drifts'. I do think posh gardeners are funny. You never hear them talk about 'drifts' of ground elder or stinging nettles, do you?

Half-hardy perennials include many fuchsias, argyranthemums (marguerites), pelargoniums (geraniums), verbenas and helichrysums, which are mostly used for container planting. These plants are true perennials in their native (hotter) climates, and can limp though most mild winters in towns (where it is a degree or so warmer), if they are given the shelter of a wall, kept fairly dry, and if their roots remain unfrosted. Even if you overwinter them in a greenhouse or porch, where they may be subjected to bad pest attacks, they have to be cut back, cleaned up and generally 'rejuvenated' in the late spring if they are to perform well the following year.

A **shrub** or bush is a plant with several woody stems coming from the base and can be anything from 6in to 20ft in height. Those sold in UK garden centres should all be frost hardy, although I have on occasion seen tender shrubs such as some abutilons and *Lantana camara* sold without a warning label to say they were tender. Some hardy shrubs may suffer some winter damage to their extremities if they are exposed to icy winds but will generally recover the following summer. Almost all shrubs need pruning or tidying at some point during the year once they are established.

A **tree** is a single-stemmed woody plant from a few feet to well over 50ft in height. Some trees (notably eucalyptus, pawlonia and some willows) can be persuaded to become almost shrub-like by being stooled each year in the spring – that is, cut right to the ground and encouraged to make several branches from their bases.

Once you have all of the above under your belt, you may read on…

CHAPTER 2
The Good Earth

How on earth, I have been asking myself (apart from printing it all in green), do you make a chapter on soil in a gardening book anything other than a deeply boring shade of brown? Considering how much time we spend grubbing about in it, scraping it out from under our fingernails and sweeping clods of it off the kitchen floor, it is amazing how little we really know or care about it. Things are looking up, however. Ten years ago, as often as not, we did nothing to our soil apart from sprinkle a bit of peat on it from time to time or empty out old growbags, or the compost from old house-plant casualties, on to the flower beds. (I know a dear old thing who for years has given her strapping six-foot camellia three old tea bags a day – on reflection, maybe she was on to something: perhaps that is how it got to be strapping in the first place). We now bandy about words like 'mulch', 'compost' and the need for 'soil improvement' as if we really understood their significance. Even the slackest among us feels a twinge of unease if we just scrape a hole in a piece of the compacted, dry, urban filth that passes for soil, bung a plant in it and splosh a bit of water about, hoping for the best.

Plants need to grow in good **topsoil** – that is, a mixture of ground-up rock particles that contain a variety of vital minerals, plus water, air, and decayed animal and vegetable matter (**humus**), as well as bacteria and micro-organisms which form natural nutrients. Plants thrive in soil that has balanced proportions of nitrogen, phosphorus and potassium (described as N, P and K on fertilizer packets). Beneath the topsoil is **subsoil**, which cannot support plant life. It is mostly a mixture of rock particles, minerals and water plus, for many of us, bricks, bits of old bike, broken china and general domestic detritus as well. I have become convinced, over the years, that an ancient English tribal rite consisted of going out into the back garden and throwing around blue and white cups and plates. So great is the volume of the stuff that I dig up that I am sure I could reassemble several tea services.

Depending on where you live, your topsoil can be anything from a few centimetres to about 50cm deep, and it can be acid or alkaline (soil over limestone or chalk is alkaline, soil over ancient woodland or marshland is generally acid). This, known as the **soil pH** (level of alkalinity or acidity), can be quite easily assessed, to work out which plants will grow well.

To further complicate matters, soil particle size dramatically affects the **texture** of the soil. It can be **clay**-based, which bakes hard, almost with a crust on it, or becomes waterlogged. Soil like this is hard for plant roots to penetrate and compacts easily if walked on when it is wet. It is generally referred to as 'sticky' feeling, but I prefer to call it 'slithery' to the touch. It is extremely hard to dig except at certain times of year when it is neither too wet nor too dry. Then there is **sand**-based and silty soil that you can almost run through your fingers when it is dry. It drains too quickly so that nutrients wash through it and it easily becomes infertile. Few of us have what every gardener covets: good **loam**, which has equal proportions of sand, clay and the organic matter that breaks down to form humus.

Whatever its basic type, topsoil in most small gardens suffers from one or other of the two following problems:

Unless it has been regularly 'topped up' with organic matter, it is thin, dusty, and infertile, having been over-cultivated for generations. Since the demise of the horse as an easy-to-come-by source of coarse, texture-improving, nitrogen-rich manure, things have gone from bad to worse. Access to the average back garden can be difficult, so even if you have a convenient source, carrying bags of muck or other goodies through the house is not a joyful task. But with little or no input of meaningful organic matter other than a sprinkling of peat (which has no nutrition in it) or the emptying out of those tired old pots and growbags, our garden soil is just not giving of its best.

The other frequent problem that arises where builders have been active is that the topsoil may have been unwittingly polluted or worse, churned up completely so that what passes for topsoil is actually subsoil, with little or no nutrients or humus in it, at all. Unless instructed to do so, builders rarely do the sensible gardening thing and, before digging foundations for walls, excavating drains or whatever, reserve in a special pile the topsoil they removed so that order (and gardening) can be returned swiftly to the site once they have departed.

While not wishing to oversimplify a very complex subject, I cannot stress enough that both of these frequently encountered soil problems can be largely overcome if you regularly fork loads of coarse organic (which means that it was once living) matter in to garden soil around plants. You should also incorporate organic stuff in to the soil by **trench digging** (see pages 74-5) where possible before planting up new beds and borders. What you add to the soil is up to you, and you should have at least a vague idea of your soil pH when you make that choice.

For me, home-made compost is the best organic stuff, but few gardens can generate enough. When I run out of home-made, I use spent mushroom compost, which is easy to come by and doesn't smell awful. In many areas, there are people who sell it from the back of a lorry and will bag it up for you. It is slightly alkaline (I save my neutral-to-acid leaf mould for my lime-hating plants), but not as nutritious as nitrogen-rich horse manure, which is also excellent if ready rotted. I generally top up my soil fertility each spring with blood, fish and bone or with pelleted chicken manure: organic-based fertilizers bought in bags from garden centres. These are balanced fertilizers with roughly equal proportions of N, P and K. If you have clay soil – you will know because it will be so hard to dig when it is very dry or very wet – you should get into the habit of adding coarse sand or grit whenever you plant or dig. This will help open up the texture and help it to drain more efficiently.

As I see it, the key is to *concentrate on improving soil texture*. Then, whatever nutrients you add in the form of fertilizers, whether they are organic or inorganic balanced fertilizers, time-release capsules or the convenient quick-acting soluble kinds, will be retained together with moisture and air. The whole root-growing environment is thus transformed.

So much for the broad principles. I feel it would be useful to look at some aspects of the whole soil subject in greater detail. Along the way we should get to understand a little more about what is meant by such things as soil fertility and fertilizers generally, compost (there's a confusing word for a start), trench digging, mulching and the much-misunderstood question of soil pH.

Soil Fertility

As I have previously mentioned, plants need the so-called macronutrients – nitrogen, phosphorus and potassium – to grow and flower well. They also need trace elements, such as magnesium, boron and copper, but I think that is quite enough science for one page. You just have to think of plants as children – needing a good diet in order to grow. Plants show various symptoms when grown in infertile soil – their leaves are paler, their flowers fewer and their growth less vigorous than their well-nourished friends. Recent research apparently shows that adding fertilizers to our gardens does not have as much effect as we would hope. I can only remember my first garden belonged to a tall house in West London. Heavily under the influence of my parents, both keen gardeners and botanists, I was dragooned into applying masses of rotted horse manure to my whole garden before they would let me plant so much as a single wallflower. As I recall we carried it in great bundles through the house, over the new carpet, slung in a pair of huge old curtains that my mother had sacrificed for the purpose. Such dedication to horticulture was not unusual in our household. A year or so later, I was standing one evening at the window at the very top of the house with my small son, watching the planes and helicopters coming in over the London rooftops. As he whooped with joy and waved a sticky index finger at an approaching helicopter, I recall vividly my amazement as I looked down at our garden. It was quite noticeable that in our plot, the greenery was two shades darker, the flowers were that much brighter, and everything was taller and more juicy looking, than in any of the other gardens in the little row of similar plots below me. All that goodness in the soil was actually visible. I don't suppose the helicopter pilots noticed, though.

Back to facts:

Nitrogen (N) in the soil is important for leaf growth. Spring lawn treatments are therefore rich in nitrogen. However, if you give flowering plants more than they need, they will produce too much leaf and not enough flower. Nasturtiums are a good example of this. If grown in poor soil, they flower much better and produce less irritating leaf growth.

Phosphorus (P) is essential for general plant health and disease resistance. Autumn lawn food is high in phosphates – but low in nitrogen. It strengthens the grass for the winter and ensures that it has a strong start in the spring, while not encouraging it to grow fast and lush just before the winter.

Potassium (K), generally referred to by gardeners as 'potash', is important for the production of flowers and fruit. A 'high-potash' feed is a fertilizer that will kick-start plants into flowering. You tend to give this to flowering containers and tomatoes from about midsummer on, once you see that the plants are starting to produce their buds.

You can test your soil for fertility with little test-tube kits and convert your kitchen for a day into something resembling a school chemistry lab. My advice is that, unless you have a growth and health problem in certain areas of your garden, it is really not worth the effort. Whenever I have gone through the motions with various students we have come to the sobering conclusion that our gardens were equally deficient in all of the three macronutrients.

General-purpose granular fertilizers

Macronutrients are traditionally applied to the garden in spring in the form of a balanced fertilizer – that is, one that has equal proportions of each element in it. During the Second World War, when efficient food production was a key factor in the national fight for survival, the government of the day developed a fertilizer – National Growmore – that has become the well-known Growmore of today. For years, gardeners have been applying the recommended 4oz per square yard around the whole garden (excluding the lawn) to give the whole shooting match a bit of a lift. Incidentally, 4oz (about 135g) is two hefty, gloved woman's fistfuls to you and me. (You don't bother to weigh garden fertilizers the way you do sugar.) Growmore (and other brands that call themselves 'balanced granular general-purpose feed' or some such catch-all name) is an inorganic fertilizer. Changing attitudes have led people to return to the traditional, organic-based 'blood, fish and bone' fertilizers that are the nearest equivalent in terms of balanced nutrients. You need less of the blood, fish and bone per square yard – approximately one fistful will do. In both cases you should fork the stuff gently into the top few inches of soil. The rain will do the rest. Another so-called balanced fertilizer is pelleted chicken manure, although the manufacturers are notably vague about the actual N, P, K content. If you don't want to use anything containing bonemeal (see page 25) and you want to use an 'organic' fertilizer, then chicken manure may be the best answer. I recently saw something called pelleted hop manure for sale in my local garden centre. I shall be trying this out next year, safe in the knowledge that although the hops were unlikely to have been grown organically, at least they aren't grown in horrid conditions.

If you talk to truly organic gardeners, they will tell you that if you add enough organic stuff to the soil at regular intervals, general fertilizers are not really necessary. But you can never know what 'enough' is, and I suspect it is more than ordinary gardeners have the time, patience or energy for. So I always add a general fertilizer in the spring, around March, and, if I am feeling diligent, again in the middle of the summer.

Time-release fertilizers

Like general-purpose granular fertilizers, time-release fertilizers also tend to be balanced. Although they are relatively new to us domestic gardeners, they are thankfully getting cheaper. They take the form of little orange capsules, the silicone coating of which starts to dissolve and release the fertilizer within only when they are damp and the temperature is sufficiently warm for plant growth. The manufacturers claim that they are effective for a whole growing season. It seems all very clever, and is an ideal way to fertilize plants in containers and window boxes, but to me seems a bit of an extravagant way to feed a whole garden. Perhaps I am just mean and old fashioned.

Soluble fertilizers

Soluble fertilizers are what you might call horticultural 'wonderdrugs' and include (inorganic) Miraclegro, Phostrogen, and so forth. They vary in their NPK content so you should take a look at the smallest print on the packaging. What they have in common, however, is the convenience and the speed with which they take effect. Using them feels almost like cheating. The point about soluble fertilizers is that they are taken up by the roots within days, are not dependent on being washed gradually into the soil. While they are very quick to hit the spot, the effect is not as long lasting. They should be applied at regular intervals during the growing season – generally once a week or fortnight. There are always good instructions on the packets.

Soluble fertilizers can also be applied as a foliar feed – plants can actually take up food through their leaves which is useful if you are short of time, and during dry weather when plant roots are under stress. The best time to do this is the early morning or in the evening, but never in the middle of a sunny day.

I wish some of the manufacturers wouldn't make their products blue, pink, and so on. It makes it feel even more as though you are giving the garden medicine. There are, incidentally, organic versions of water-in fertilizers based on seaweed extract that it is claimed are just as good. Don't get the evil brown liquid on your clothes, however.

A word of advice: if, like me, you have a dreadful habit of leaving fertilizer boxes out in the rain, or hidden under a damp bush for cardboard-eating snails to munch, you may well find it helpful to decant the contents of your boxes into old plastic lidded tubs or cartons. Do not forget to make a note of the dosage and any other useful instructions, and write the information on the tub (plant label marker pens do the trick), otherwise you will kick yourself. I know these things.

Specific fertilizers

There are also, as I have already mentioned, soluble and granular fertilizers for specific tasks or plants – roses, lawns, bedding plants, tomatoes for example – each with a different NPK balance, which you can see by looking at that small print on the backs of the packets. You can also buy nitrogen, potash and phosphate fertilizers separately for specific nutrient deficiencies. It can all get very complicated if you let it.

Bonemeal

Until recently, no gardener worth his or her salt would be without a bag of bonemeal – organic, slow-release phosphates applied to the soil when planting and considered to essential for long-term plant growth and health. Even in the wake of the BSE scare of the late 1990s, bonemeal is still on sale, many gardeners use it, and there seems to be no clear directive not to do so either from the government or from the Royal Horticultural Society.

It is certainly evil-smelling stuff as you might expect, and I have always taken great care to wear gloves when handling it and not to inhale it. There are other forms of phosphates – superphosphate (inorganic) and rock phosphates (organic) that you can use instead. But again, in theory, if you use enough organic stuff on your soil, you probably don't really need to use a separate phosphate fertilizer anyway. As is often the case, it is a question of personal choice, not a question of right or wrong.

Soil pH

There are two facts about plants that seem to stick in people's minds, even if they claim to know little else about them. One is that 'clematis needs shaded roots', and the other is that 'camellias need acid soil'. The subject of clematis I will deal with later (see pages 58-64), but it is amazing that, in a whole section on soil, I have as yet barely touched on the one thing about the subject people seem to think so important.

The acidity or alkalinity of soil (its pH value) is generally thought to be something to do with soil fertility, but it is not. It is really a question of some plants being fussy about the pH of the soil around their feet. If it is unsuitable for them, they are unable to take up nutrients from the soil and become sick. It has to be said that relatively few plants are extremely fussy, and that the vast majority of plants can cope with, or adapt to, their site.

Soil pH is measured on a scale of 1 to 14. Soil with a low pH (under 7) is known as acid. Soil with a high pH (over 7) is known as alkaline. Soil above chalk or limestone can be very alkaline, while the soil on land that is, or was once, heathlands and deciduous woodlands tends to be acid. If you really want to know your soil pH, then you can buy little test kits similar to those for soil fertility. Remember that you would have to take several samples from various parts of the garden to get a true picture.

It has always struck me that the hysteria about soil pH is a bit of a storm in a teacup. You tend to know if you live in an area where the soil has an extreme pH, one way or another, by looking at what grows often and well in neighbouring gardens. Furthermore, you can often work out a plant's likely preference by thinking about where it came from originally. A plant such as sage grows naturally in thin soil on rocky hillsides (alkaline), while a camellia comes from leafy deciduous woodland (acid). Thus you would be on a hiding to nothing to attempt to grow rhododendrons (a group of plants known to be pH fusspots) if you lived in the middle of the totally unsuitable chalk downs of the south of England, for example. Plant reference books will usually tell you if a plant has extreme preference for acid or alkaline soil, as will plant labels.

The problems, I think, arise with pH when you have soil that is not extreme, so that you can grow just about anything, but a few plants (almost always the acid-lovers) start to complain. Certain acid-loving shrubs – the camellias and rhododendrons I have already mentioned – show their distaste for too-alkaline growing conditions by developing yellowing leaves with prominent green veins (classic symptoms of iron-deficiency chlorosis). This can be treated with an iron tonic, such as Sequestrene, or by occasional feeding with a liquid feed, such as Miracid, which treats the soil with iron and feeds the plant at the same time.

All evergreens (including camellias and rhododendrons) have an alarming habit of dropping loads of leaves at the end of the spring after flowering, just as they are putting out their new green shoots. Generally the leaves go bright yellow before they drop. This is entirely normal and it is an evergreen shrub's way of having a little 'autumn' on the quiet. If you have any doubts about chlorosis, look at the newest leaves. If they are a good green, everything in the garden is rosy, as it were.

I should also add that chlorosis is not just a symptom of iron deficiency. In my slightly acid soil, I had a languishing magnolia that should have been quite happy with my soil pH, but shrugged off all attempts to cheer it up with the addition of iron as described above. A local gardening friend had seen the problem before and suggested that the young tree was suffering from a lack of magnesium (one of the trace elements also necessary for plant growth) and told me to spray its leaves with Epsom salts. Hey presto – it now thrives. Only, as luck would have it, a late frost wrecked its wonderful flowers in its subsequent first truly happy spring. Sometimes I hate gardening.

To sum up: go with the flow. Acquire a rough idea of your soil pH by looking around you at neighbouring plants. If you must grow plants that are bound to be unhappy with your conditions, grow them in containers or specially prepared raised beds in ericaceous compost (see below). And remember that not every yellowing leaf in the garden is down to lack of iron as a result of low soil pH.

I have compiled a short list of shrubs that have specific pH preferences:

Shrubs for very alkaline soil: artemisia, brachyglottis (formerly senecio), buddleia, caryopteris, ceratostigma, cistus (some), cotoneaster, deutzia, euonymus, forsythia, hebe, helianthemum, lavender, philadelphus, phlomis, potentilla, *Rhus typhina*, rosemary, rugosa roses, salvia, santolina, thyme, weigela.

Shrubs for very acid soil: acer, amelanchier, azalea, camellia, cornus (some), enkianthus, eucryphia, fothergilla, hydrangea, kalmia, magnolia, mahonia, nyssa, pachysandra, pieris, rhododendron, skimmia.

Compost

The word compost is a pretty useless one, if the truth be told. Corrupted from the French *compôte* and absorbed into the English language, it is one of those words which is meaningless on its own, and has to be qualified at length lest it cause considerable confusion to us poor gardeners. Woe betide he or she who confuses home-made compost with soil-based or even peat-/peat substitute-based materials using the same name. You absolutely mustn't get your John Innes Nos. 1, 2 and 3 composts muddled up. What is horse manure compost composed of? What makes one compost 'organic', and another not? And what, then, is tree- and shrub-planting compost? Or ericaceous compost? Is the stuff they call multi-purpose compost truly what it says it is? First, we will look at the goodies – 'gardener's gold' – that we can make ourselves.

Home-made compost   Free food for soil is a subject close to my heart. For years I have been trying to convince new owners of small gardens that it really is worth saving all their trimmings, clippings and sweepings, and storing them in an orderly manner in one part of the garden. While it would be rather grand to call these garden waste bins 'compost heaps', it is possible to rot organic matter down after a fashion and then to return the resulting brown stuff to their garden soil, in however small a quantity. This is essentially what composting is all about. Once you have acquired the habit of composting your garden waste, instead of throwing it out, you will find it comes as second nature to scale the whole operation up if and when you get a bigger garden. I find it all wrong to use one of those garden vacuum cleaners that seem to take up residence in the sheds of even the smallest of gardens, unless they are used specifically to collect and shred garden debris in order to rot it down, and so return it to the soil in composted form. I was under the impression that a lot of us garden obsessively in order to get away from the Hoover…

As I said earlier, in order to thrive plants need organic matter in the soil. Most of our gardens are deficient in organic matter owing to over-cultivation over the years. The best way to improve the health and vitality of your garden is to increase the amount of organic matter in the soil. Think of hedgerows and grass verges: they are fertile, vibrant and full of flowers, year after year, as a result of their own greenery dying down and rotting back into the soil to feed everything. It stands to reason that by scurrying around trying to keep our gardens as neat as new pins for twelve months of the year, and throwing out all the old vegetation with the domestic waste, we are robbing our soil of its own natural food, which is, after all, free.

What sort of container do you need for composting? Broadly speaking, there are two main types on offer. Firstly, there are slatted wooden ones, some of which do not work very well because the slats are too widely spaced so the compost dries out and doesn't rot down very well without a bit of fussing, mixing the compost around and even watering it. They look pleasing, however, and are therefore easy to live with. Secondly, there is a variety of plastic ones on the market, some of which are insulated to speed up the composting process. They work very well but most of them are ugly and therefore not so easy to live with.

How do they work? There are two ways of rotting things down. One method uses the natural heat resulting from large volumes of greenery being put all at one time into a sealed container. If you have a shredder this method is ideal. I put all my hedge trimmings and shredded shrub prunings into a black plastic bin that looks like a dalek without its sink-plunger. The bins heat up amazingly fast and I can get a load of useful well-rotted stuff from them in about six months. The other, more usual method involves the activity of moulds, bacteria and worms, and so forth, and takes up to a year to yield anything worth using. You can speed things up a little by using a biological compost accelerator such as Biotal.

How do you prevent a 'slow' heap from becoming either a stinking mass or a pile of twigs? The 'slow', or 'cold', method of composting works as follows: ideally the heap needs to be at least a cubic metre in volume; if it is any smaller, the process takes even longer. Furthermore there should really be only about a 10cm layer of any one thing (such as grass clippings, snipped-up prunings or kitchen waste) put in at a time. You should occasionally turn the outside edges into the middle of the heap, add the odd layer of garden soil and perhaps a compost accelerator. You should check that the heap is not too dry in the summer, especially if you have hidden it under a tree or behind a shed, and occasionally water it. In winter, you should cover the heap with a piece of old carpet underlay, or similar, to stop it getting too wet. If you are going to use kitchen vegetable waste, make sure that it is not contaminated with meat otherwise it could attract rats. It may all seem like a bit of a palaver, but it works, and once the compost heap is full to the top, the fun bit starts. You turn the top bit over, add a layer of soil, climb on top of the whole thing and jump on it to compact it. To my chagrin, my neighbour actually discovered me doing this – in my nightie.

To find out if your compost is ready, you will have to scratch around in the base. Take the top (unrotted) few inches off, bag up the good stuff beneath, and return the top bit to the bottom of the heap and start again. Ideally you should have two heaps next to each other, so that one can be filled while the other finishes rotting.

Remember that if a compost heap is working well, it doesn't smell foul – just a bit earthy. If it starts to stink, this means it has gone wet and sludgy in the middle – usually because there are too many grass clippings in it. Mix in some straw, if you can get it, or shredded newspaper to open it up a bit.

Is there anything that can't go in the heap? Don't put the roots of perennial weeds such as bindweed and ground elder in a heap in case they start to grow and infest the compost. Similarly, you should try to avoid putting in weeds that are in flower or have gone to seed. Woody trimmings should be snipped up into 5-cm lengths. I suppose I should advise against putting any unwanted bulbs in there as well, as I am constantly amazed at the number of daffodil bulbs that pop their leaves out between the slats of my heap in the spring.

One final thought: I keep an old flowerpot on the ground by my heaps. In it I chuck all the old bits of wire, old plastic plant labels and other non-biodegradable dross that gets kicked endlessly around most gardens. There is nothing more annoying than having to pick out old plant labels from otherwise beautifully made compost. If nothing else, it comes as an unwelcome reminder of just how many plants you have killed over the years and how much they cost you.

After all this, what do you use home-made compost for? I have referred to it as 'gardener's gold' and, together with leafmould (see below), it really is the best, the ultimate soil conditioner. Unfortunately, we never seem to have enough. I use mine as part of a planting mixture, for improving my vegetable patch (which is organic), and for improving the soil in containers and tubs. If I had tons of the stuff I wouldn't ever use anything else.

Leafmould
You can make compost from falling leaves so never chuck them out, and please, please never burn them. Fallen leaves are Mother Nature's other free gift to the gardener. If you have a bit of space, pen them up in a chicken wire cage and leave them to rot. Dead leaves rot down in a completely different way to green garden waste and are best kept separate in this way. They take much longer to rot, but a year or two later you have a wonderful supply of this crumbly brown stuff known as leafmould, that looks, feels and

smells divine. Even if you do not have the space, bag up your leaves (make sure they are damp), puncture the bags and hide them for a year or more where you can't see them, under evergreen shrubs or behind the shed.

Both home-made compost and leafmould are ideal for **mulching** – which is another of those words that needs a bit of explaining.

A **mulch** is a layer of material, generally but not always organic, that is spread over the surface of the soil to perform various useful functions. Organic mulches such as home-made compost, rotted animal manure, leafmould, mushroom compost, composted bark or cocoa shell help to keep down weeds, retain and conserve moisture and protect plant roots from frost. They also help to feed plants as they break down into the soil. However, these foody mulches, as I call them, have to be applied much more thickly than you think in order to do an efficient job. Ideally they should be 8–10cm thick, and applied or topped up every year in the spring, when the soil below is thoroughly moist. Inorganic mulches such as gravel, black plastic sheeting or planting membrane, conserve moisture and suppress weeds. Fine gravel round the necks of plants that hate British winter wet – alpines and so forth – helps to stop them rotting away.

I would love to say that I mulch all my beds and borders every year, but I don't, because it is enormously expensive and time consuming to do. But I do mulch all newly planted shrubs and plants with as rich and foody a mulch as I can muster, particularly those planted in the spring, in order to give them a good start in life. But if it is practicable to mulch everywhere, then you should. Over a period of time, as the mulches rot down even further they become part of your topsoil, and do an immense service to all your plants.

A note to slack gardeners: it is not a good idea to put greenery – fresh lawn clippings or shreddings – directly on to flowerbeds as a mulch. While it acts as a good moisture-retentive layer, green waste can heat up as it starts to rot, scorching plant stems. And it actually takes nitrogen out of the soil it is lying on as part of its rotting-down process. Nor it is a good idea just to leave piles of leaves where they get blown in the autumn on to flowerbeds to rot *in situ*. All they will do is act as duvets for a rampantly hungry slug and snail population throughout the winter. You will lose your dormant delphiniums and your hostas will appear almost pre-shredded, sure as eggs.

Composts in bags

As I indicated earlier, the word compost covers just about anything brown and sold in thick plastic bags at garden centres. First of all, we should look at potting composts, or planting mediums, the sort of stuff you buy to put in plant pots, seed trays, tubs and the like.

Potting composts Potting composts basically come in two forms: soil-based or peat- (now commonly peat- substitute-) based.

Soil-based composts   These are frequently sold as 'John Innes composts'. The name John Innes refers not to a manufacturer but to a formula that defines the proportions of soil, peat, sand and fertilizers. There are three types: John Innes No. 1 is a light peaty/sandy mixture fairly low in nutrients, suitable for starting off seeds and cuttings. It is, helpfully, often called 'John Innes Seed Compost'. No. 2 is slightly more 'soily' – suitable for potting on young plants. No. 3 is grittier and richer – for mature plants and long-term container-grown shrubs. The main problem with using them for large containers is the weight of them when they are wet.

Peat- or peat-substitute-based composts   These do not contain soil, and are, therefore, lighter to handle. They are often labelled 'multi-purpose' because, in theory, that is what they are. I find there is a huge drawback to using them. Once they dry out, they are almost impossible to wet thoroughly again. We all have, in our time, tried to revive tragic little plants of this or that, temporarily abandoned in a corner, the compost dried to a crisp and shrunken within the pot. When you water the pot, all the water comes shooting round the side of the compost, which remains as dry as a bone – unless you spend five minutes of your precious time doing a handstand on the thing in a bucket of water while the compost gradually plumps out again. If you have to use peat-based compost for reasons of weight, you should consider adding to it one of the gel moisture-retaining agents sold for the purpose.

A word about peat. There is an on-going rumpus in the gardening world about the removal of peat for commercial purposes, and most responsible gardeners have stopped, or almost stopped, using it. There are substitutes – many previously 'peaty' composts now contain coir, bark or some such, and the gardeners seem unable to agree as to whether they are as good as, or better than, peat. You can chose how 'green' you want to be, but certainly you should never add peat to your soil in bulk as a conditioner. It has no 'food value' whatsoever. There are far better alternatives – such as my beloved mushroom compost – that do.

What to use? An enormous amount of research goes on to try to prove that this or that compost gives the 'best' results – you can hardly open a gardening magazine without seeing a series of photos of pelargoniums or something similar in plastic pots ailing to a greater or lesser degree because of the failings of such and such a product. It is, as you might have guessed, absolutely not the purpose of this book to précis the latest findings of all these back-room boffins. I will just stick my neck out and describe what works for me.

For seeds and cuttings I use peat-free multi-purpose compost with added sand to improve drainage. I have also used a straight mixture of 50/50 peat and sand (with no added nutrients since the plants do not need feeding at this early stage).

For potting on (the next stage on for small plants) I use multi-purpose compost. I have parched a few loved-ones to within a millisecond of death on more than one occasion, but on the whole I am quite caring and fussy about small plants that I have propagated myself, and they get the best of my (generally scatty) attention.

When preparing serious containers for long-term residents I generally mix three parts John Innes No. 3 (the chunky one) with one part multi-purpose compos', to lighten it slightly and to increase its sponginess. If I haven't any multi-purpose compost to hand, I add one part of home-made compost (if I have enough to spare) or use mushroom compost, which does a similar job. I find that John Innes No. 3 on its own tends to become rather rock-like when it settles in the container. A newly planted-up big container full of fresh compost of this kind has enough nutrients in it for about a couple of months or so. Thereafter you will have to start feeding. What I would definitely not use for container planting is ordinary garden soil or bought-in bagged topsoil – the first because it would contain weed seeds and soil pests, and the second because it is such an unknown quantity, or, should I say, quality.

It goes almost without saying that you should buy any bagged compost from a source that has a quick turnover of such products, since bagged up composts definitely deteriorate with age. They should be just very slightly damp with a nice earthy smell. If, when you open up the bags, the contents are very wet or green with algae, take them back to the place you got them, put on your best assertive smile and get your money back.

These growing mediums should not be confused with all the other things in bags, a selection of which is described below. I include this caveat only because the husband of one of my more recent students once mulched his entire garden to the depth of three inches with a well-known brand of multi-purpose compost. Apparently he did think at the time that this was a rather expensive way to fertilize and mulch his garden. Indeed it was.

Compost for lime-hating plants *Erica* is the Latin name for heather – a lime hater. Hence the rather odd name of the compost. Ericaceous compost is lime-free and is sold mostly for use in containers and raised beds where you intend to grow rhododendrons, camellias, heathers and others in that tribe of lime-haters. I also use it together with a little bonemeal when planting them in the open ground if I have no neutral-to-acid compost such as leafmould available.

Soil improvers and planting composts

Blended horse manure compost This comprises horse manure mixed with hop waste, straw, peat or wood-shavings with bonemeal added. It is good to plant with. The fact that it says 'compost' on the bag means that it is well-rotted and ready to use, unlike horse manure proper, which must be at least six months out of the horse and smell-free before it comes anywhere near plants.

Chicken manure This is organic, highly smelly, very rich in nutrients, but not as bulky as horse manure compost. Remember it is the bulk of these composts that is needed to improve our soil as much as the goodies within them. The same goes for anything containing cow manure. I would use these as spring-time top dressing fertilizers.

Shrub- and tree-planting compost This is what it says it is. If you have no home-made compost, leafmould – the 'gardener's gold' I referred to earlier – or well-rotted horse manure, this is the next best thing. Often it is recycled green waste, as produced by an increasing number of local councils, and can also be used for general mulching along with those mentioned below.

Barks and mulches

Composted bark This is not very foody but is an excellent soil bulker and has a low pH, so it is good for acid-loving plants. Other bark products (coarse chippings, for example) make a good but rather untidy mulch but take for ever and a day (up to five years to be precise) to break down into the soil and provide something useful for the plants.

Cocoa shell This makes efficient mulch but smells of rather sickly chocolate. I personally think it looks horrid until it has broken down and become incorporated into the soil. But as a mulch it is tidier than bark chips. I have also known cocoa shell to make a small (greedy and stupid) dog extremely sick. I am sure there is something to be said here about barks and bites, but I can't quite think what.

CHAPTER 3

Shrubs — including Corrective Guidelines for Habitual Abusers

I feel sorry for shrubs. I think they are going through a bad patch, historically speaking. For years our Victorian and Edwardian forefathers looked upon them with affection, reverence even. The 'shrubbery' was a calm and serious place for contemplative perambulation, a place to relax and unwind after a hard day's Empire building. They were sombre places where you could rest your eyes, so frequently dazzled, in other parts of the garden, by garish bedding schemes and, as garden fashion shifted, blazing displays of roses.

There was another burst of enthusiasm for shrubs of a totally different kind after the Second World War, a burst that lasted well into the 1980s. Shrubs and dwarf conifers were seen as labour saving, and the idea of low-maintenance gardening took hold. The legacy is with us today. Little blue and gold conifers planted as eye-catching features now loom monstrously over many a suburban home, blocking out the light and turning the surrounding soil into a dark, lifeless desert. Shrubs with sharply contrasting foliage of plum, lime-green and grey lean mop-headed and oversized in countless once colourful mixed borders. Having squeezed out the peonies and smothered the phlox, they just sit there, their congested branches half-heartedly snipped at from time to time by nervous owners anxious not to do anything to upset the overwhelmingly leafy status quo.

And now what are the New Gardeners up to? Forgive me if I have not caught up with the fad for stainless steel garden structures and feature walls made out of broken council paving stones, or whatever. I am hoping that the whole phase will pass by swiftly before I am obliged to join in. The only breaking of new ground that goes on in my garden involves a spade and a wheelbarrow as I intensely dislike this endless quest for instant gratification in gardening which seems to be leaving shrubs out in the cold.

Shrubs take time and patience. They don't really look any good for at least a year or two and they eventually grumble if they are grown in pots. So they are definitely not 'here today and gone tomorrow' plants – unless you manage to kill them, that is. And yet I strongly believe that anyone who has any sensitivity for the way in which gardens relate to our natural landscape must appreciate that shrubs have to form the backbone of any garden worth the name. They form, if you like, the stylized hedgerows in the stylized meadows that our gardens generally represent. I know it is not quite the same if you are gardening in an inner city courtyard or in the Scottish highlands, or on treeless chalk downs, but I am sure you get the general drift. Peace and space: that is what we need from our gardens, and to my mind that has to involve at least shrub or two. I am probably expressing the views of a horticultural dinosaur, but so be it.

Most of us, faced with brand new or sparsely planted gardens with no 'soul', know instinctively that a tree and a few large shrubs will make all the difference. But how do you go about it in a small space? Many of us, conversely, have gardens where the existing shrubs have taken over, and are both out of sorts and out of shape. We really need to thin them out and learn how to prune before the garden can move on.

This is, therefore, how I will tackle the subject of shrubs. How do you chose them, how do you plant them, and what do you do with them once they have become established? There is no magic formula, because our tastes and our gardens differ so wildly. But hopefully the guidelines I set out will help you to think about the whole business of shrubs in a more optimistic and constructive way. First the practical stuff:

Choosing Shrubs

I simply can't do this for you since this is not that kind of a book. But there are loads of books out there that do. There are some basic pointers you should take into account.

Sun or shade?

It is really important to know whether shrubs need sun or shade before you set your heart on them. Approaching things from the other direction, you ought to understand what is meant by sunny and shady, when applied to gardens.

Few small gardens are really sunny, simply by virtue of the fact that they have a two- or three-storey house on one side of them. Boundary fences and walls can also create this sort of roof-less shade in which plants get quite a lot of light from above, but not all that much direct sun. All in all, there will probably be only one area, sometimes inconveniently in the middle of the plot or in one corner that you call your 'sunny bit'. However much you may fib to yourself, this may only get a few hours of sun anyway. In winter it may even get none at all. Hardly the scorched Provençal hillside, and yet we all fantasize about growing lavender, cistuses and all that sunny stuff in inappropriate places. Crazy. Grown without pretty much full sunlight, otherwise stunning cistuses will lean and stretch across the garden and look gaunt and ugly, however much you tie them up and try to prune them into shape.

In addition to limited direct sunshine, most gardens have areas that are dominated by nearby trees, giving dappled shade to whole tracts of garden at various times of the day. As leaf canopies thicken up as summer progresses, these areas can then become virtually no go areas for other plants. Come the spring, however, when the trees are leafless and the whole garden bathed in light, we all forget about the problem and start planting the barren areas anew. There are, it has to be said, an awful lot of ways to waste your time and money in gardening! I will address the problem of planting under trees later in this chapter (see pages 41-3).

So think carefully when choosing a shrub. It is not just a question of light and shade; but also the natural habitat of the plant. Does it originate in the dry, airy, sharply-draining hillsides of southern Europe? Does it require the temperate moisture of its native New Zealand, or is it a woodland plant, used to the protection of deciduous trees, with a leafy acid soil in which to put its roots? Plant books will tell you all this, and it is important information to assimilate. Plants work best if you can plant them in conditions similar to those they are used to in the wild, and they can cause immense problems if you try to resist going with the flow. An azalea will look as sick as a dog on a stony, sunny bank, and a curry plant will wither to nothing in the shade of an oak tree. Furthermore, it should go without saying that plants that come from the same neck of the woods, as it were, associate well together. Think how jarring on the eye would be a border accommodating both lavender and rhododendrons.

Variegated shrubs, with green/yellow or green/cream leaves are loved by some (me included) and loathed by many. They have been bred from naturally occuring freaks of nature, and are always less vigorous than their green relations. Inserted into gardens in moderation, they can brighten dull corners and lift the dreary days of February considerably. Beware rogue green shoots that may appear as the shrubs get bigger, and remove them at source or the shrub will eventually revert to plain green. This is particularly problematic with the Euonymous family, in my experience.

A word of warning: Golden-leaved shrubs, both evergreen and deciduous, need particular conditions. They should be planted so they do not get the midday sun. Otherwise they bleach out (as in the case of *Choisya* 'Sundance') or scorch and go brown and hideous (as in the case of *Philadelphus coronarius* 'Aureus'). If you already have these shrubs and they are in the wrong place, move them if at all possible. Otherwise they will always be an eyesore.

Buying Shrubs

As we are all increasingly aware, there has been a major change in the way people garden in the past twenty years or so. Shrubs used to be bought bare-rooted by mail order in the winter, and had to be planted before they acquired their leaves. Now they are generally supplied in 1-litre plastic pots in which they have spent their entire lives since they were taken as cuttings in a nursery. They are generally at their best if they are about eighteen months old, after which they can become pot-bound (which means their roots become cramped) and can deteriorate if not potted on straight away to a larger pot or planted out in a garden. You can plant them at any time of the year, as long as you take the necessary precautions of watering and keeping a general eye on them for the first few months. Evergreen shrubs, many of which are tender, are happier if they are planted in the spring so that they can find their feet and get established before their first real winter.

Watch out for plants sold in 2-litre pots (with an appropriately hiked up price) that are just very old 1-litre pot dwellers that have simply been dumped in fresh compost to cover the weeds and mossy mess in the top of the old pot. This practice is not as prevalent as it was, because we are all a lot smarter, but it still happens, I assure you.

It is not necessarily a good idea to home in on the biggest shrub in the batch at the garden centre, since it may have been under the most stress, having grown too big for its boots as it were. It is better to look for the chubbiest-looking plant with strongest new growth, the best leaf colour, with no sign of pest (snails or aphids, for example) and no roots trying to escape out of the bottom of the pot. These are the real health indicators. And one other thing: if you are like me, you will pull all the plants out on to the path to chose the right-shaped plant for the situation you have planned for it. Plants find their own shape eventually – obviously – but you don't want to start off with an ugly duckling in your little brood. Remember to put the rejects back or the manager of the garden centre will be after you with a broom handle.

Increasingly, the giant horticultural chains of garden centres sell us 'wonder plants' (my name for them). These plants are somehow spotlessly uniform, pest free and in perfect condition. There is little to chose between a batch of twenty or so of the same thing. I find the sight of them depressing, although I know it is supposed to represent 'progress' in gardening – in the same way that straight cucumbers and perfectly uniform-sized legs of lamb are supposed to represent 'progress' in food. Gardeners should make sure, however, that these plants are properly 'hardened off' and that they will be able to cope with the variable weather conditions to which they will be exposed once they leave the cosseted environment of the garden centre. In my experience, these perfect plants can go downhill before they go up, as it were.

Whatever you do, bone up on the shrubs you want before you go shopping. None of us can make proper shopping lists for plants and the acknowledged weakness for impulse buying is half the fun. But, before you buy, you really should know if that innocent little marvel you tuck into your trolley on the way to the checkout will turn out to be a 2-metre hooligan within two years, or whether it will languish behind the choisya (or whatever), with which you imagine it could look so good, and never be seen again.

Garden centres generally have someone, somewhere, who is knowledgeable and can advise; they also often have a lovely big dog-eared plant book under the counter that you can dip in to if needed. Failing this, I think we should all make a concerted effort to break the British mould and *talk to other customers in garden centres*, instead of wheeling our trolleys around, whispering nervously to our partners or frowning silently to ourselves. We can learn from each other's experience. It is, after all, what you are supposed to be doing as you read this book.

I must give a little plug here for a reference book, updated every year, called *The RHS Plant Finder*. This is a list of plants with a directory of where they can be bought country-wide and it is invaluable if you are trying to find an obscure plant. *The Plant Finder* CD Rom, now available, is packed with additional plant information. I should also mention that at least one of the major garden centre chains (the purveyors of the 'wonder plants' mentioned above), runs a plant search service, and will get hold of plants for you that they do not normally sell. I think they should shout a bit louder about this admirable service.

How big should they be?

If you are starting with a sparsely planted garden or part of the garden, buy at least one bigger shrub or small tree to give a sense of height. This is altogether encouraging and makes you feel a lot better about spending so much money. Indeed, it may bite into the budget a bit, but it will cover more naked soil as well. I am not, on the whole, an advocate of the 'fill a juggernaut with mature trees and plant a jungle' school of gardening, partly because it is a bit of a cheat, but mostly because it is one hell of a risk. Very large shrubs sometimes don't establish very well at all, chiefly because their root system is already mature within their enormous pots. However, just one or two splendiferous specimens can lift the whole game.

Inexperienced gardeners have great problems getting to know the **relative heights** of plants, and this is made far worse by the fact that garden centre shrubs are all, for convenience, generally about the same size as each other. Again, plant books will help a lot, as will reading the generally informative labels on the plants themselves. Some plants are tortoises and some are hares, and there is no way round this problem. You just have to use your loaf when spacing the plants and acquire a bit of grown up patience. Becoming a dab hand at transplanting is also important.

Evergreen or deciduous?

Remember that a garden will give you more to look at for longer throughout the year if you include some evergreens. Thirty per cent of the total is the figure often bandied about;. *at least* thirty per cent, I would say, preferably more. The real winners are evergreen shrubs that have good flowers as well. Most are familiar players such as cistuses, choisya, the many hebes and such, and there is nothing wrong with that. There is no point in getting sniffy about them just because everyone grows them. Every garden needs its solid, reliable, multi-function work-horse shrubs. All the rare and vulnerable stuff can come later, when you know what you are doing.

What else should you look for?

Especially if you have a small garden, try to chose shrubs that have more than one of the following things going for them: colourful or otherwise dramatic leaves, interesting winter stems, scented flowers, evergreen leaves, good autumn tints, bright berries. For example, if you are limited in space, it would be foolhardy to plant one of the huge philadelphuses (gaunt and ugly bushes whatever you do with them, but with those heavenly white scented flowers in June that evoke the smell of childhood summers). You could try planting the variegated version (*Philadelphus coronarius* 'Variegata'), the golden-leaved version (*Philadelphus coronarius* 'Aurea'), the fairly compact *Philadelphus microphyllus* or even the little dwarf *Philadelphus* 'Manteau d'Ermine'. But not the big chaps, not in a small space anyway.

Another example of this sort of choice is with cornus (often known as dogwood). These wonderful foliage shrubs (the flowers are nothing much to write home about) are also loved for their red winter stems. They really look their best seen from a distance, in mass plantings in huge gardens, where they are cut to ground level at the end of the spring to create a whole new crop of shoots for the following winter, but they have a place in small gardens too. The plain green-leaved one (with really bright winter stems) is, well, just plain green in the summer. The ones to grow, I think, are the coloured-leaved varieties, *Cornus alba* 'Elegantissima' (green and white) or *Cornus spaethii* (green and yellow). And don't cut them down completely in the spring, like 'big gardeners' do, unless you want to create a very strange hole in the garden structure. What worked for me with cornus, in addition to a tidy-up and shape-up each spring, was to cut out one or two stems from near the base of the plant in the middle of the summer. The new shoots that grew towards the end of the growing season were a good fresh red, the shrub didn't get over large, and the garden retained its 'shape' all the year round.

These are just two examples of shrubs that have more than one function, offering you a lot in one go. It is very often a question of leaf colour, but there is also the question of a plant's growth habit. This is where careful research, label reading and a touch of Latin help a great deal. A final word or caution on this subject: beware of *Ceanothus thyrsiflorus* 'Repens'. It may look to you like the answer to a maiden's prayer – a small ceanothus (most of them get huge very quickly and provide nervous pruners with an annual nightmare). The 'Repens' bit of the label means 'I am going to lie on the ground like a sulking hippo when I am not flowering'. You have been warned.

Planting Shrubs and Trees

It may sound a bit grand, but it really does help to use a wheelbarrow, especially if you have more than one shrub to plant. If you haven't got a barrow, then a thick plastic sheet on the ground where you are to work is the next best thing. Into the barrow or on to the sheet put about the equivalent of a bucketful of organic stuff – mushroom compost, home-made compost, rotted manure or a shrub planting compost.

Dig a planting hole for the shrub, about twice the size of the pot in every direction, and add the soil that comes out of the hole to your pile of planting compost in the barrow or on the sheet. If you are going to use it, sprinkle a large handful of bonemeal on to the pile of soil and compost and mix the lot together. If you are not, use more organic stuff as explained previously in the chapter on soil (see pages 27-30).

Put about a third of the resulting planting mixture back in the hole and fork it about to incorporate it into the soil at the bottom. De-pot your shrub, having first made sure it was sufficiently damp by soaking it in a bucket of water until no air bubbles come out of the pot, and it feels nice and heavy. You could put soluble fertilizer in the water if you are feeling in a lavish, nurturing frame of mind.

If there are any roots coming through the holes in the bottom of the pot that are dry, brown and dead looking you can cut them off. If they are damp, fresh and pale, try not to damage them. If the shrub was badly pot-bound – that is, if the roots look congested and 'tortured' in to the pot's shape – you could gently loosen the odd one with a finger. Roots are extremely delicate things, however, and much frantic picking can do more harm than good. It is a difficult situation on which to give advice; ideally you should try to acquire plants that are not in this condition.

Snuggle the roots of the shrub down into the soft soil/compost in the planting hole. Make sure that the junction between root and stem will end up at the same level as it was when potted (in other words, that the hole is not too deep or too shallow). If there is a problem with this, start all over again. If not, begin to put the contents of the barrow back into the hole around the plant, firming very gently as you go. When the roots are about half buried, water the whole area and let it drain away. Finish back-filling round the plant, firm the area with your boot (or slipper) and apply an additional mulch of organic stuff. You should not need to water again for a week or so. Should there by anything left in the barrow or on the plastic sheet, it can be rolled over into the next job.

Additional planting tips

Don't use bonemeal if you are the owner of a daft dog, who will try to dig up your plants thinking he has buried last night's dinner under them. Foxes will do the same. If you feel your soil could do with it, use superphosphate or rock phosphate or a balanced general fertilizer, such as Growmore, which is not quite the same thing but will do.

If you are planting in turf (a tree perhaps), take off a circle of turf first, and bury some of it upside down under the plant. You will have to dig a deeper hole to accommodate the extra bulk, but it is worth it. The old turf will rot down *in situ* and will act as splendid fertilizer for a few years. The plant should grow like the clappers.

If you are going to need a supporting stake (not hideous bamboo), put it in as you plant the shrub or tree. If you leave it till later you may well damage roots. Use proper tree ties or several thicknesses of twine tied loosely as a temporary measure (it will only last a year).

If you are planting at the 'wrong' time – in the summer, for example – and the soil is dry at the bottom of the hole you have dug, fill it with water and let it drain a couple of times before you put in the compost/soil mixture. If the water takes a whole day to drain away, break up the bottom of the hole again, put in some grit or gravel, and add more grit to the planting mixture – you probably have clay under your soil.

If you are planting at the 'right' time, in the autumn or spring, and the hole is dry at the bottom, think twice about the site you have chosen.

Transplanting Shrubs

While no serious gardener can possibly advocate playing chess with their shrubs on a regular basis, there is no doubt that learning how to transplant major players in the garden is a vital skill, acquisition of which gives great confidence. We all over-plant, to a lesser or greater extent, and shrubs invariably get overcrowded. We also change our minds, want to try out new combinations and ideas, and it would be only half the fun – and incredibly expensive – if we had to chuck out mature shrubs all the time.

Moving something after a year is easy, since the plant's roots will barely have moved out of the original planting hole and the soft compost you provided for it. You just have to go through the motions all over again, watering the shrub well before you start and trying to disturb the roots as little as possible. Generally the shrub doesn't even notice and its growth is barely checked. Moving young shrubs around too much is not to be recommended, since they never really get going – and the garden will look restless because of it.

Older shrubs need greater care. The best time to transplant mature deciduous shrubs is in the winter when they are leafless. However, I have recently succeeded in transplanting a 2m x 2m deutzia in midsummer, which proves that nothing is impossible.

I have my greatest success with evergreens in the very late summer or early autumn, so that they have time to recover before the winter cold, and will start to grow properly again as soon as spring comes. They are trickier than deciduous shrubs since they will usually wilt for a week or two, which will inevitably freak you out. It makes sense not to move them when it is likely to be windy, or frosty, or brilliantly hot and sunny.

If you are transplanting a shrub that is really large, start by cutting it down by up to a half. Whatever time of year it is, it will recover from the inevitable shock of losing some of its roots if it does not have to support all its old top growth. It also makes the physical business of moving it easier – especially if it has thorns.

Drizzle a hose in to the ground at the base of the shrub overnight two days before you intend to transplant. (The root area should be damp but not mushy.) Start to dig vertically down around the shrub, remembering that roots will be spread out from the main stem about as far as its branches extend. You probably cannot realistically hope to avoid cutting the outermost roots, but you should still be aware of what proportion you will be damaging.

Once you have dug around the shrub as deeply as you can go, try gently rocking it to get a feel for where the deeper roots are going. You will probably then have an idea of how large the new planting hole should be, which you should then go and prepare – following the guidelines given for planting new shrubs. What you must at all costs avoid is digging up the shrub and leaving it lying around with its roots exposed while you dig out its new home.

Lift the shrub out of its old site – it may well mean cutting one or more big roots – and onto a plastic sheet. Make sure the damaged root ends are cleanly cut off with no rips or snaggy bits that could rot and cause future problems. Then drag the plant to the new site. Check the new hole is the right size. It *must* be deep enough. Make sure that when you put the shrub in the new site it is 'facing' the right way and looks harmonious with its neighbours. This sounds silly, but if you have ever got this bit wrong, you will know what I mean.

Remember when back-filling the soil and compost that you must make sure there are no air pockets under the roots. Use your hands. Tread the shrub in well and mulch thickly.

Keep a close eye on the patient, and it should, if deciduous, burst in to life happily in the spring – although you may have lost a year's flowers because of the cutting back. Water it very well every two or three weeks in the growing season of the first year. Evergreens will inevitably wilt, even if it is not sunny. Depending on just how brutal you were and how big the shrub was, it will either take weeks or months for the shrub to return to former glory. Or it may even die on you, but at least you had a go.

Pruning Shrubs

When it comes to pruning shrubs – as I am afraid it always must eventually – gardeners divide themselves into two camps.

There are those who, at the first whiff of spring, flex their muscles, thrust back their shoulders, grasp those Christmas-present secateurs and launch themselves into the garden. Three hours later they return, having 'tidied things up' for the year. The garden, maimed but generally not fatally wounded, takes months to recover. The ceanothus, *Clematis montana* and shrub roses don't flower, and the choisya is reduced to something resembling a set of antlers sticking out of the ground, but at least the pathways are clear and nothing hangs over the lawn to interrupt the progress of the mower. These people, caged lions in urban gardens, dream of moving to the country where they can plant lots of trees and train their sons to be the next generation of axemen gardeners, giving them plastic swords with which to chop off the heads of the rhododendrons when playing with their little friends.

Then there are those who love the romance of the overgrown jungle or the 'cottage garden look' and blench at the sight of a pruning saw or the thought of consulting a pruning manual. These are the gardeners who will happily plant a Russian vine to grow up a wisteria or a 'Kiftsgate' rose to go over a shed. They plant *Lavatera* 'Barnsley' in groups of three and can't bear to cut them down in spring because they were 'so good last year'. When the whole garden threatens to strangle them in their beds, they cut their way into the tangle with a pair of kitchen scissors, put a bench in the resulting hole and call it an arbour. When it all gets too worrying, they put their houses on the market while everything is in flower so no one can see the mess and then get the hell out – a bit like selling the car when the ash tray is full.

Do not presume, however, that there is a gender divide. I am the product of a mother who, now partially sighted and with a dickey left arm, is still pruning for England at the age of 90. My father, on the other hand, adored trees and shrubs until he died, planting them with gay abandon – often with little prior discussion, slap in the middle of my mother's herbaceous bits – and then just leaving them. They became the subject of acid discussions over numerous Sunday lunches as they grew more and more unsightly and out of control. Nor did the trees and shrubs look any better. My father, I am convinced, had no idea how to prune, despite his great botanical knowledge.

What follows is a serious attempt to make pruning easier for the romantic ditherers and to put a curb on the most uncontrollable axemen. There are no pictures to help you. I am using no diagrams of perfect shrubs (that look nothing like your own sad wrecks) with little black marks across the branches to show you where to cut. Trust and concentrate. Then go and look at your shrubs and see if it all begins to make sense.

All mature garden shrubs – those over two or three years old – need some kind of pruning to keep them looking good. Pruning is largely a matter of common sense – the application of a few bendable rules to suit your particular requirements. If you employ outside help to do your pruning, as often as not it will be a disaster since many 'gardeners' resort to a scorched earth policy because they do not understand these rules. Even if they do, they often do not have the intimate knowledge that is needed of either your plants or the site to adapt the rules to the best advantage. There are three main methods of pruning:

1   Cutting back hard;
2   Thinning out;
3   Spur pruning.

1 Cutting back

This is what you do to LATE-flowering deciduous shrubs, those that *start to flower after midsummer* on the end of shoots produced during the current season. Examples are: buddleia, lavatera.

In very early spring (late February perhaps in the south of Britain, later in the north) cut all branches back to a woody framework, which should remain virtually unchanged over the years once the shrub is mature. The size and height of the framework depends on a) how much the shrub grows each year before it flowers and b) at what height you want to see the plant flower. For example, *Buddleia davidii* grows approximately 4–5ft in a year and flowers from the tips of its branches. If you wanted to keep it as small as possible, you would prune annually, to a framework of about 1ft in height. If, however, you wanted the bush to hide an 8-ft high garden shed, you would only cut the front branches to 1ft, staggering the framework so that the back branches would be cut down to about 5ft. (They look wonderful treated this way, with those pointed scented flowers stretching out on the end of long supple branches. You get that heavy honey scent at nose height and upwards: lovely.) Shapes and sizes of shrubs can be quite precisely stage-managed in this way.

Cutting back is also an effective way of dealing with *very* overgrown shrubs that need drastic treatment, whatever their flowering period. However if you cut back EARLY-flowering shrubs in February (as opposed to the LATE-flowering group above), there will be few, if any, flowers that year.

Less vigorous LATE-flowering shrubs, such as potentilla, lavender and hypericum, do not need drastic cutting back every year. A 'haircut' with the shears each spring is sufficient, and at the same time, you can cut out at the base any dead wood from the middle of the shrub to tidy it up.

All cutting back should be followed by heavy feeding, mulching and so on.

2 Thinning out

This you do to EARLY-flowering shrubs, which flower on side shoots coming off the previous season's growth. Examples are: winter jasmine, forsythia, ceanothus, rosemary and philadelphus. Since these shrubs *only* flower on year-old wood, the aim is to control growth while encouraging production of more new shoots to carry flowers where they are wanted the following year. It is a subtle operation, but not difficult if you do it *immediately* after flowering has finished – which could be February in the case of winter jasmine, or July in the case of philadelphus.

Thinning out should be done in two stages:

a) Cut out at ground level all very old (the thickest and most gnarled), diseased and damaged wood. 'One in three branches' is often quoted, but it depends on the type, age and condition of the shrub you are working on. When you are thinning out a neglected bush for the first time, you will probably need to use a small pruning saw. It will be hard work. What you are aiming to do is open out the base of the bush so that new, vigorous stuff has room to develop and grow up through the older stuff.

b) Shorten stems which have borne flowers back to a point at which there are some strong buds showing, *even if those stems have started to put out new growth at the tip*. The shoots you are removing would be naked and ugly for most of their length the following year if you left them to grow on, while the buds and shoots to which you cut back will carry *next year's* flowers. What you are aiming to do is keep the shrub roughly the same size overall, while ensuring the maximum numbers of branches carry good flowers.

If you are working on a very large shrub, keep standing back and looking at the overall appearance of the bush. The basic branch pattern should not alter much and the shrub should generally look much better and slightly smaller immediately after pruning, with the bright young shoots that will grow to carry next year's flowers in greater evidence.

If you are timid with this thinning out the shrub will be too blowsy by the end of the summer. This is when the problems really start, with the temptation to give the shrub a short back and sides as you tidy things up in the autumn, resulting in the removal of many of the new shoots already carrying flower buds for the next spring.

Mastering the art of pruning EARLY-flowering shrubs is one of the most important jobs in a small garden, where space is generally limited and every shrub has to earn its keep to the full.

3 Spur pruning This is what you do to wall-trained shrubs or climbers where space is limited. The aim is to check growth severely whilst persuading the plant to produce as many flowering shoots as possible. It is quite difficult to do and even harder to explain, but in my experience few gardens contain more than one or two plants in this category – wisteria and *Chaenomeles* (Japanese quince) are the most common examples.

In early summer, cut back all new (long and whippy, in the case of wisteria) shoots to within about six leaves of their starting point, saving only those shoots needed to create part of the permanent structure. Another crop of new shoots will then be produced during the rest of the growing season from the axils of the remaining leaves, and these should be similarly cut back in the autumn or early winter. At the same time, the shoots that were originally cut back in the summer should be shortened even further, leaving about three buds from their bases. Any other whippy growth that is still in evidence after you have done all this should be shortened to a few inches.

I do recommend getting help with wisteria pruning if yours is a large specimen. It is all very well being brave and self-sufficient, but it is really dangerous counting all those leaf buds up a ladder in a force nine. My parents used to have a vast wisteria with a mind of its own all over the front of their house. Dad used to cut the phone wires just about every time he did the pruning. He hated doing the job, and I think he was trying to tell my mother that professional help was needed, bless him.

A rather unorthodox combination of SPUR PRUNING and THINNING OUT can be used for some early-flowering, over-vigorous shrubs – such as forsythia, which, for some reason, always seems to be planted where there is not enough space for it – at intervals throughout the growing season. If the growing shoots are trimmed back by about a third every five or six weeks, they will still produce enough compact new growth to give a good display of flowers the following spring. It is worth experimenting once you understand the basics.

Some exceptions to the rules

Evergreens Evergreen shrubs grown chiefly for their foliage effect should have their branches shortened and thinned out and some of the oldest growth removed in March. Frost-damaged shoots should also be cut out at this time. Very vigorous shrubs or hedges can be cut again in July. Evergreens that are also grown for their significant flowers generally flower in the spring (*Viburnum tinus* and *Choisya ternata* are two examples). They should be cut back after flowering, either quite hard every other year or gently every year. If they are not pruned, you often get a surprisingly good second flush of flowers in the autumn, so the alternate year approach is more rewarding.

Late-flowering evergreens (such as hebes and brachyglottis/ formerly senecio) should only have damaged shoots and tired flower heads removed, until they get too big. Once this happens you have to cut them right back in early summer and you will get nothing – except lush leaf growth – from them until the following year. If you don't want brachyglottis to flower, treat it as an evergreen pure and simple, cutting it back each spring.

Early-flowering shrubs grown for berries (such as pyracantha) need sensitive handling. Prune out half of the shoots that have flowered immediately after flowering, to encourage new growth for next year. Leave the other half to form berries for the blackbirds!

Hydrangeas There is no single rule since there are so my different types. The common mop-heads and lace-caps flower best from younger wood, and at the very least you should take out wood that is more than two years old from the base every spring. At the same time, prune down shoots that have flowered once to a pair of fat buds (somewhere in the top few inches of the shoot), but do not touch the young shoots that have not yet flowered. *Hydrangea serrata* and *H. paniculata* can be cut down to a framework each spring once they are two or three years old, since they flower well on new wood.

Lavender Technically speaking, this is a late-flowering shrub, but it is one that gets very woody and ugly after only a few years. It should be trimmed twice. Immediately after flowering, remove the flowers together with the stalks and about 5cm of each shoot; during the remainder of the summer the bush will re-grow and become a good rounded shape. The following spring prune the bush again, this time taking off about 10cm (it depends on the variety, if it is a big lavender, take off more). Do not cut right down into the old wood – that is, below the little grey whiskery shoots that you can see just emerging from the woody stems. If you do, the lavender will not flower well that year. If you have a very old lavender that is gnarled and ugly, replace it (you could try taking cuttings from it), unless of course you like the rather exotic shape of it. Formal lavender hedges should be neatly pruned to look good. I just love to walk slowly along an old path edged with dark purple lavender, heavy and humming with bees in the heat of the mid-day sun. It is, to my mind, one of the best garden experiences.

A Final Observation

Shrubs are not the only plants to which the 'early-flowering' and 'late-flowering' labels apply. The fog of confusion surrounding the subject of rose pruning can be somewhat dispersed if you realize that while hybrid tea, climbing and floribunda roses flower on the current season's growth, and must therefore be pruned in the spring, ramblers and shrub roses flower on the previous season's growth and should be dealt with after flowering. Similarly, there are early- and late-flowering clematis. I will deal with these in subsequent sections of the book, but I thought I would just throw this in as food for thought.

CHAPTER 4

Walls and Fences and Things

Walls and fences to most people mean 'climbers', but growing climbers is not always the best solution to covering walls and fences and hiding eyesores. I shall attempt to explain why.

For a start, climbers climb. Up and up. Many are woodland and hedgerow plants that, by various different means that I will describe later, climb up host trees until they reach the sun – and pollinating insects – and then they flower. The host plants provide them with nutrients in the form of decayed fallen leaves, protect their young growth from strong, drying winds and also shade their far-reaching roots, which need cool moist root-runs and plenty of space.

Now consider the average garden fence or wall, desperately in need of 'clothes', either wind-swept, blisteringly hot and sunny or dank and shady, invariably with dismal soil or indeed none at all at it base. You will then see why we gardeners so often run into problems.

Wall Shrubs

I will start this section by ignoring the actual climbers for a bit and looking at the alternatives, the shrubs, often referred to as 'wall shrubs', that do well with their backs flat against a vertical surface, perhaps tied lightly to it. Over these you have much more control than a tangle or of interlocking climbers. At least you have once you understand more about pruning.

House walls that are naturally warm, especially sunny ones, provide the most interesting planting opportunities. Favourites include ceanothus – all sorts, mostly blue, mostly spring-flowering, mostly evergreen, *Cytisus battandieri*, not evergreen and flowering a smitch later, with silvery leaves and stubby racemes (dangly bits) of pineapple-scented yellow flowers, *Rhamnus alaternus* 'Argenteovariegata' a good workhorse-type variegated-leaved evergreen that is eminently trimmable and adaptable. Likewise several pittosporums with all sorts of leaf colours from gold through variegated to dull plum. Some shrubs that you don't associate with height achieve remarkable climbing feats if tied up lightly. Brachyglottis (formerly senecio) can surprise you this way, as can *Phygelius capensis*, with its upside-down-looking orange bottle-shaped flowers in late summer: most exotic.

Shade is, as always, more difficult, and sun-lovers planted against shady walls will never flower as brilliantly as they would with a bit of sun, and will lean and stretch towards any light source. But with nourishment, adequate water and a bit of support, you can coax something out of spring-flowering chaenomeles (Japanese quince), or use the strong shapes of mahonia or *Fatsia japonica* (the castor oil plant) against a contrasting background. I have seen dear old brachyglottis (see above), choisya and rhamnus trying really hard against shady walls as well.

In all cases, remember, if you are going to tie woody stems back on to a wall – or on to any kind of support – you must use proper shrub or tree ties, double or treble thicknesses of lightly tied garden twine. Even bits of plastic-coated electrical flex will do (as long as it is not white!) I have even known people resort to using old tights. Never, ever, use garden wire, even as a 'temporary measure'. The chances are you will, like me, forget to go back to re-do the job until the branches in question have been severely cut into by the wire, and untold damage has been caused. Humiliating stuff.

As with so many spur-of-the moment gardening jobs, the fag of having to go and get the right tools or materials for a job is more then outweighed by the sense of virtue and well-being that comes upon you when you know that the job has been *properly* done. This is the sort of frightful stuff our grandmothers taught us, and it has taken me a surprisingly long time to find that it is true.

I really like wall shrubs. They add depth to the boundaries of a garden, and if you are lucky enough to have good shrubs coming over the fence or wall from a neighbour's garden, you can even make they boundary 'vanish' by planting the same things on your side. It may be just a personal quirk, but I find the sight of a larchlap fence covered by solitary clematis rather soul-less, even when – perhaps especially when – smothered in bloshy blooms the size of dinner plates. What I really, really like to see is a series of well-ordered wall-trained shrubs with climbers growing within and between, and even all over them, but not smothering them. It is not so very difficult to achieve if you chose your plants carefully and don't succumb to the temptation to grow too much, too close together in order to achieve an 'instant' (dreaded word) result. Furthermore, you have to understand the different needs and habit of the plants involved.

But there is something about climbing plants that captures the imagination of all gardeners, and leads them astray.

Climbers

These are very much the icing on the gardening cake. Allowed to ramble seemingly unaided up walls and fences, through and over other plants and features, carefully chosen so as to harmonize or contrast perfectly with their hosts, they create a magical effect – especially in small gardens where both drama and detail are so important.

So much for the fantasy. In reality, what we generally end up with is an ill-thought out mish-mash of climbers that need different pruning care, planted in the wrong place with little or no support apart from each other, cantilevered out from the over-burdened garden fence and causing serious damage in the neighbourly relations department. It can quickly become an uncontrollable nightmare. So here are some things you should know about them:

Firstly, *choose carefully* when planting new climbers. Rampant climbers such as *Clematis montana*, *C. armandii*, the dreadful evergreen honeysuckle and wisteria really do need a lot of space and very sturdy support *before* they get going. As previously mentioned, they are really designed by Mother Nature to go up trees and stay up there, or even wander from tree to tree without let or hindrance for years. If you have the space to let them do this, lucky you. In smaller gardens, however, they can overwhelm and kill other shrubs (generally, of course, those belonging to your neighbour).

If you grow smaller climbers up into existing mature shrubs, remember that the pruning rules apply to all shrubby plants, including climbers. For example, do not grow a group B clematis that needs minimal winter or spring pruning into a December-pruned climbing rose.

Secondly, *climbers need a good, deep root run.* That is why most of them do really badly in pots. This is an undeniable fact and one that even experienced gardeners fail to come to grips with until they have squandered a small fortune. It is also a heart-breaking fact, since so many of our gardens have areas with blank walls and fences and no soil to plant in at their bases.

The only sensible advice in these circumstances is to try to move heaven and earth and paving stones or whatever to create a good planting area – coming out from the wall or fence by at least 2ft with really good soil the depth of at least 2ft. It will probably be necessary to replace completely the foul stuff that you find under the paving stones or concrete which you have removed. Alternatively you could build substantial raised beds with proper drainage, taking care, of course, if a damp-proof course is involved.

Here is a useful tip for hopeless girlie gardeners. Always try to remove paving stones or lay bricks when there is a builder nearby, even if you know that they are fully occupied installing a tricky RSJ or gloss-painting the front door. You will undoubtedly have the club hammer or knitting needle, or whatever it is, gently taken from you and you will be shown just how it should be done. I have not actually tried bricklaying in my nightie, since I have always had excellent results in this department even when wearing filthy jeans and a torn wax waistcoat, looking relatively capable to boot. There are still, bless them, plenty of traditional blokes out there. By the way, thanks Dave, the climbers are doing a treat.

If there truly is absolutely no alternative, then grow non-rampant climbers in huge containers – half-barrels even – and remember that:

a) a climber will only go up as long as it can go down, and

b) that it must never, ever be allowed to dry out.

Use a container that is as non-porous as possible and does not conduct heat well (wood is good – if it is unglazed, terracotta should be lined with plastic). Plant in John Innes No. 3 compost with time-release fertilizer granules. Cover the top of the soil with pebbles or cobbles to retain moisture. Do not be tempted to plant anything else in the tub or pot with the precious climber or it will have to compete for water and food. If you absolutely must, then stand other pots of ivies or pretties on top of the pebble layer in the barrel. This will jolly it up a bit visually, disguise the enormity of the container below and provide a source of second-hand water and nutrients by draining into it when you water them. Every year or so, remove the pebbles, scrape away the top few inches of soil and replace them, adding more food as well. With this gold star treatment and much effort, you will probably succeed.

In any event, try to avoid shoe-horning climbers into dry bits of scrubby soil where they have to compete for food, water and root space with their intended hosts. This is especially important if the hosts are already well established and will be robbing their new young companions of all the necessities of life from day one.

If you are planting a climber – a rose or clematis, say – to go up a tree, try to plant it as far away from the trunk as possible. I find that a branch pruned from the host tree, placed on the ground and leant against the tree's lower branches, to which you loosely tie the climber, provides the most natural way to 'lead' it upwards. Remember, you will have to look at whatever support you give for a long time. In my view nothing is worse than an alien-looking bamboo cane in this situation. Once up in the lower forked branches of the tree, the climber will most likely find its own way up as nature intended, but you should check things from time to time and, if it is struggling, lend a helping hand by wrapping a piece of chicken wire around a branch or tying stems in loosely.

When planting near trees and shrubs, always, always, improve the soil in the planting area massively, digging down as deeply as you can, and mulch and feed for the first year while the newcomers are finding (or perhaps I should say burying) their feet.

One last thing on the subject of planting climbers: You have been dreaming idly for weeks – thoughout an entire summer, maybe – of seeing cascades of flowers of some heavenly scrambler tumbling elegantly from top to bottom of some otherwise unremarkable tree at the end of the garden. You know how it is; we all do it. Come planting time in the autumn (you don't know how you managed to show such self-discipline and wait this long), you drive thirty miles to the only nursery in your part of the country that stocks your wonderful whatever-it-is. You rush home – knowing already where you are going to plant it. Start digging. Shock horror. You manage to dig two feet down and still the soil is full of tree roots, dry as dust, frightful. You do what you have been told. Fill the hole with water – go off and do the crossword, drink a gallon of coffee in sympathy, whatever. More shock horror – an hour later the water hasn't drained. Oh woe, oh woe. Must be solid rock or clay underneath. Take my advice, plant your treasure somewhere else. You have just hit on the 'planting site from hell' and the plan will never work. I write as one who knows.

Wherever, whatever and whenever you plant your climbers, they will only behave the way they should if you provide them with the *right kind of support*. If you take a good look at various types of climber, you will see that they actually have totally differing methods of scrambling upwards and benefit from differing methods of support.

I will mention roses only briefly as they are dealt with elsewhere. I should mention, however, that in the wild they use their thorns as a means of scrambling up trees and things and, in gardens, ramblers are quite happy to climb trees this way. In the confines of the ordinary garden, climbers and ramblers need to be tied to supports. They should never be poked behind retaining wires or woven in to trellis. The wires will soon damage the shoots and the trellis will be wrenched apart as the rose expands.

We are all familiar with **twiners**, such as honeysuckle, jasmine and the dreaded wisteria (have you really got room for this seductive giant?). In fact it is amazing how many people think that *all* climbers do it this way. Such plants initially need vertical support. They should be untwined very carefully from the cane they have been grown up in the nursery. The stems should then be fanned out (or whatever is appropriate to the site) and encouraged to go up parallel vertical wires. You get quicker results this way. Remember you only get one shot at it, because before you can say 'Jack Robinson' your climbers will have shinned up whatever you provide for them – often things like phone wires and drainpipes that are, shall we say, less than ideal. Unless you want the whole shooting match to land on your head after a storm in a few years' time, use proper heavy galvanized wire and vine eyes.

It is not just about being sensible just for the sake of it. The plants do – and look – a lot better. I once made the mistake of leaving a honeysuckle twined around itself and a bamboo cane, only fanning out the top growth. After a few years the bottom two feet looked like a massive twisted piece of rope with a tortured cane splintered and broken in its middle. It was truly ugly and can't have done its best that way.

Petiole climbers such as clematis and *Solanum jasminoides* 'Album' use their leaf stalks to help them scramble about, forming what I call 'elbows' where the leaf stalk (petiole) joins the leaf and making a kind of knot around their support. (Incidentally, the blue solanum – *Solanum crispum* 'Glasnevin' – doesn't do the same thing at all. It barely supports itself at all, and should really be called a 'scrambler' rather than a climber. It needs to be firmly tied up and rigorously pruned.) Petiole climbers need a fairly fine mesh to grow up unless they are climbing up other plants. Oddly enough, the gauge of wood in ordinary garden trellis is too large for them, and they can end up flapping about in anything more than a gentle breeze, which will naturally slow their progress. Fairly coarse chicken wire (which you can get in either dark green or just plain galvanised metal) stapled or nailed on to fences, walls, sheds and so forth, and on the back of trellis or even wrapped around rustic poles, is surprisingly invisible. It enables the plant to create a firm base from which to ramp ever onwards and upwards.

Climbers such as ivy and campsis are **clingers** once they get going but need rough brickwork into which to stick their small aerial roots. They 'take' very slowly on dry, warm wooden fences and detest creosote and most other wood preservatives. If you buy a big ivy on a bamboo cane from a garden centre, do not expect the growth it already has to somehow start to stick to your walls. Once you have planted it you should take the ivy right off the stick and bury the stems in the (improved) soil along the base of the wall you are trying to cover, so that only the leaves remain visible above ground. It will make numerous new shoots along the length of each stem and these will then march up the wall at an amazing pace, giving a wide area of coverage in a remarkably short time. It will certainly be a whole lot quicker than trying to anchor the stems to the wall or worst of all, just leaning the plant, stick, plastic ties, staples and all against the wall and hoping it will find its own way in due course. Anyone blushing?

Tendril climbers, such as grape-vines and other ornamental vines, will grab at any support, turning their tendrils into little springs. Take a close look sometime: it is one of nature's marvels. They thrive best with a combination of vertical and horizontal wires about 18in apart, forming a grid. If you want them to look smart and formal, you train them carefully on to these wires so that they make a permanent woody framework to which you prune back every winter. If you don't, they will just lurch around, grabbing anything they can latch on to. Chaos but rather nice unless space is limited. Vines live a long time, so their support wires should be strong and able to last for up to 400 years or so. You have been told.

Another annoying fact about grapevines is that, unlike most other climbers, they cannot just be tidied up if they send out too many undisciplined shoots in the wrong direction during the early summer. The flow of sap is so strong that if you cut or injure the new shoots they 'weep' uncontrollably for weeks. Instinctively, you think that they will weep to death, though apparently this is not the case. It is just not very nice to sit under a vine-covered arbour and be dripped on. All in all, I regard grapevines in small gardens as a bit of a fantasy plant for the dedicated and knowledgeable.

There are climbers – Virginia creepers and various relations – that stick their little hand-like **suction pads** into crevices and rough stonework. They can just about climb up fences unaided, but on these and on smooth rendering they prefer help with waterproof sticky tape or a bit of Blu-tak until they start growing strongly. If the wind blows them off their support thereafter, they generally manage to climb straight up again, although you may have cut bits off first.

A final thought on supporting climbers. Fortunately, few of us have totally new gardens with naked walls and fences to clothe from a standing start. But often, because of deaths or disasters or building works or a combination of all three, boundaries and surfaces in our gardens become free for planting. In the light of experience, I think I would now immediately cover the surface with coarse chicken wire, with maybe some horizontal wires as well, even before I decided what to plant. This would give me the greatest flexibility in my choice of plants, as well as that aforementioned warm feeling of having for once done a really grown-up job.

All this is very well if you are planting anew, or have plenty of space, but what about that appalling mish-mash to which I referred earlier? The answer is glaringly simply: decide to cut things right down, preferably remove completely the trouble-makers, and let the rest start again. I know, I know, it sounds so simple, but when you stand in your garden and look at your *Clematis montana* waving at you from the top of the neighbour's cherry tree and triffid like branches of another neighbour's grape-vine trying to strangle you as you speak while the ground is littered with the mildewy leaves of simply everyone's so called evergreen honeysuckle, it all just seems too much. But I promise you, if you actually take a weekend out of your life and do it, you will never regret it.

In certain circumstances, great care should be exercised – particularly when you have just acquired a new garden. I am reminded of the sad but hilarious tale told me by one of my London students. Blitzing the massed and matted climbers and over-grown shrubs on her boundary in late winter, she came across a seemingly dead limb of something massive with no sign of life on it anywhere. Having been told to overcome her wimpish tendencies where pruning was concerned at all costs, she cut. It was such a massive thing she was forced to fetch the pruning saw. Two doors down the road, the 'owners' of a *Clematis armandii* in full, heavenly flower were stunned when the whole thing wilted for no apparent reason.

Generally, though, hard pruning never hurt anyone, or anything. I am sure the aforementioned *Clematis armandii* did not die, and that it leapt back into life in its real owner's garden, for a while, anyway, until it got the wanderlust again. There are certainly times when brutal and radical first-aid pruning is absolutely unavoidable. I write as one who only last year had to cut down to within two feet of the ground an ancient *Clematis montana* two weeks *before* it was due to flower because it was in the way of some builders (not Dave this time). It is back up there flowering as I write. Unstoppable.

Clematis – Simplified at Last

I think I should devote a special little section to clematis, because they give so many otherwise confident gardeners the habjabs.

The general gist of complaints is that:

a) they always die on you and

b) if they don't die, they get out of hand and you don't know what to do with them.

Let us look at the first problem: untimely death. I find the key to clematis is the planting and treatment in the first year. Most deaths occur because plants are not treated with enough TLC in the early stages, but once established clematis generally go from strength to strength.

Timing

For a start, clematis prefer to be planted in early autumn or late spring – in other words when the soil is still warm from the summer or starting to warm up in the spring. Nurseries and garden centres get in good supplies then, so the choice should be wide. If you buy them at other times, you will be offered the plants all the sensible gardeners have already rejected.

Planting method

Clematis really *do* need to be planted in absolutely wonderful soil that has been dug deeply and enriched in advance. Try to find a specimen that has as much new growth near the bottom as possible. Young plants tend to be supplied in tall slim pots (because clematis have deep roots) and the hole you dig should be at least twice the depth of that pot, and about three times its width. In the hole should go half a bucket of 'good stuff', such as mushroom compost with a little bonemeal, or home made compost or whatever you use for shrub planting from the garden centre. Fork it all around to incorporate it into the surrounding soil and sprinkle some more to be mixed with the soil that will be packed back around the plant. Then fill the hole with water and let it all soak away. This takes longer than you think. (This is all fairly standard information for planting anything.)

The next bit is important. Place the unpotted clematis in the prepared hole, and make sure that the hole is deep enough so that the first five or six centimetres of the stem of the plant will be *under the soil* once the soil/planting compost is put back round the plant and it has all been firmed down.

The reason for this is that clematis shoots and stems are thin, brittle and vulnerable. Should there be a problem with clematis wilt (see below) or, as is more likely, snail or slug damage at soil level, dormant buds on the stem below soil level can shoot out from the healthy root system and all will not be lost.

Watering and shading the roots in the early stages

Having been deeply planted in a thoroughly exemplary manner, the clematis should be watered slowly and given a liquid feed if it is planted at the start of the growing season. Then you should give the whole area a really thick, deep mulch, and tuck in a few slug pellets (if you use them) around the stems, and leave the plant well alone.

As the growing season advances, drench the plant every two weeks or so (depending on the weather) with a gallon of water, temporarily pulling away the mulch and applying it very slowly so that moisture reaches the plant's root system and doesn't just wash away over the surrounding soil. The last thing you want to do is water too little, encouraging the roots to grow upwards to the surface of the soil where they are likely to be baked in hot weather. If you think you may have been a little foolhardy in your choice of planting site, sink a plastic pot or drink bottle (face down in the soil with its bottom cut off) adjacent to the new plant, and fill it with water a few times each week.

It is surprising how many gardeners – even complete beginners – will rightly tell you that 'Clematis roots should be shaded'. However, few do it adequately. I have seen so many sad little plants dried to a crisp – most of them still tied to their garden centre canes – against blisteringly sunny walls, with stems emerging from soil that looks as though it was imported from the Arizona desert, and with nothing more substantial than a couple of bits of broken terracotta flower pot placed pathetically on the ground in front of them to 'shade the roots'.

'Shading the roots' actually means planting the clematis so that it is protected from the mid-day sun by the foliage of other plants – preferably shrubs and preferably evergreen. If clematis are planted against brick walls, which act as vast storage radiators, it means more than this. For a start, the clematis should be planted at least 45cm from the wall. 'Shading' can mean placing a large, thick paving stone over the base of the plant on top of its mulch, or it can mean placing a container of other plants in front of the clematis – a good idea, because the clematis will be 'watered' by proxy. It does mean making a big fuss, but fortunately only for the first year or two. Once clematis have got their feet firmly down under, you can be much more lackadaisical. A nice, thick, foody mulch every spring should be all that is required.

Clematis wilt

Even the best efforts of the most dedicated gardener can all come to nought when, just as the plant is really getting cracking and shinning up it's support at a rate of knots, one shoot after another wilts. Steadfastly ignoring all attempts to revive it with copious drinks, the poor plant hangs lifeless in the wind, finally turning up its toes and dying. The dreaded clematis wilt has struck. Or has it? Some recent research has shown that a substantial number of so-called clematis wilt deaths are in fact caused by slug and snail damage at the base of new plants (hence the need to buy plants with more than one emerging shoot, and the advice about slug pellets at planting time).

Whatever the apparent cause of the problem, the course of action is the same: Cut the plant down, make sure it is well watered and well mulched and check for slugs and snails in the vicinity. Then just wait. Whatever the cause of 'death', if the roots are sound the plant will shoot back up. Perhaps it will not be immediate, but by the end of the growing season there should definitely be signs of substantial life in the form of new strong shoots. Don't relax the slug and snail vigil.

What you absolutely must not do is dig the plant up and replace it with another one, because if the cause *was* clematis wilt, then the virus in the soil can transfer itself to the new plant and the whole thing could happen again. If the clematis re-emerges, it will thereafter be resistant to wilt (a bit like measles in that you can only get it once). If your clematis, having recovered, keels over yet again you know it was pest damage or just plain shoddy treatment on your part in the first place.

We will leave death and destruction behind and move on to another problem for would-be clematis growers.

Support

I have already described various ways in which to support climbing plants, but I think it should be stressed that clematis do need careful treatment in the early stages if they are to perform at their best. I have also said that clematis prefer to ramble around on other plants and seem to do best this way. But however you grow them, you should put in some fairly fine-gauge support for them to latch on to for the first few feet of their growth. The bamboo cane and those loathsome green plastic ties and staples that they come with should be regarded as very temporary and should be removed as soon as suitable alternatives have been put in place and firmly grabbed. Equally loathsome, in my view, is that semi-rigid plastic mesh sold (in brown, green or white) by the metre as 'clematis support'. Chicken wire looks much better and lasts just as long.

So much for new clematis. What, now, about the ones we already have and don't really understand?

You may have noticed on their labels and in books about them, that the powers-that-be divide clematis into three broad groups which they call, helpfully for once, A, B and C, or 1, 2 and 3. They are divided thus partly because their pruning methods differ and this is supposed to simplify things for us. Understanding the broad groupings may, as well as enabling you to chose appropriate types for whatever function you wish the clematis to perform, help you to work out what to do with the ones you already may have. As with everything, there are all sorts of sub-divisions and bits in brackets to make us all think we can't understand, but basically it goes like this:

Group A (or 1) This group is made up of vigorous species and hybrids that flower on the previous season's growth from January to May the next year.

Popular examples that we have mentioned above are the rampant *Clematis montana* and *C. armandii* (which is evergreen). There are also some more refined and delicate ones such as *Clematis alpina* and *C. macropetala*, with small flowers and ferny leaves.

How do you prune them? It has to be said that the whoppers look best unpruned, and they should really only be grown in places where they can grow to at least 5m in height. But if it is necessary to limit their growth and, let us be realistic, few of us have the sort of space where it would not be, you should cut off the first crop of long new shoots that are produced just as the clematis stops flowering. More long shoots will subsequently be produced, but the growth rate will have been reduced by about a third. These new shoots will carry the next year's flowers, and should therefore not be messed around with later on in the summer. Every few years it will be necessary to have a proper sort out and hack back after flowering. However hard you prune them back, they are very hard to kill.

A word of warning about *Clematis armandii* in small gardens. I have already mentioned my student who 'pruned' one that had decided to move house to delight her neighbours two doors away. There is something else that upsets people with small gardens who try to grow *C. armandii*, thinking that an evergreen clematis unbeatable: *C. armandii* does not drop its old leaves, so when it marches onwards after flowering, producing a wild array of the juiciest new growth to carry the next year's flowers, it will leave behind a vile display of long dangly 'everbrown' leaves to delight you. The answer is to prune it quite hard, right from the first year, or to somehow weave the new shoots over the old growth and tell yourself you will 'sort it out next year'.

Clematis macropetala and *C. alpina* are altogether more well behaved, and like nothing better than to be sent up small garden trees or over arches and bowers where they will stay, performing beautifully with little or no pruning at all. And they produce fluffy seed heads to boot. Perfect.

Group B (or 2)

Group B (or 2) These are the tricky beasts that get us all in a panic. These are the gorgeous ones that flower their socks off in the middle of summer – the real show-off ones. In addition to their midsummer spectacular, they have a lesser production in about September, often with slightly different, single, flowers. They, like the Group A ones, flower on growth they put out during the previous year.

Examples of this group are numerous. However most people know 'Nelly Moser', with its mauvy-pink flowers with each petal barred with a deeper pink, and 'The President', a mauvy-blue and so frilly that it looks like crêpe paper.

How do you prune them? It has to be said that the pruning of this group is complicated, and therefore usually not done at all, which is why so many gardeners, having planted these really showy clematis, end up with an ugly, unproductive bird's-nest. The bird's-nest is all the more annoying if you have grown clematis from this group among roses or shrubs that need to be pruned at a different time. It can all lead to serious lethargy in the pruning department.

What you should do is cut Group B clematis back to about 9in from the base in the second spring after planting, to promote branching growth. I appreciate that it is well-nigh impossible to bring yourself to do this dreadful little task. After all, who in their right minds, having dug, watered, mulched, fed, fended off pests, put up chicken wire, dragged around paving stones and generally been to hell and back for the sake of one small clematis, is going to be happy to cut the whole thing down to 9in, especially when it has finally made it in to the big league and is about to offer you some flowers to brag to your friends about? But this is what you have to do, and if you grit your teeth and *do* it, you will be rewarded, I assure you, with a chunkier and more floriferous plant ever more.

Subsequent cutting back is not nearly so heart-stopping. You just trim out dead stems and cut back by about one third in late February, bearing in mind that if the plant is cut too dramatically at this time, early flowers will be fewer and smaller. Take great care during this early trim not to cut bits that look totally dead but actually carry substantial amounts of growth on their ends. After the plant has done its stuff, remove the dead flowers and a short length of the old flowering shoots to encourage the production of a second crop of flowers in September. What you are doing here is removing tired growth, similar to pruning early-flowering shrubs. But you also want that additional late summer crop of flowers, so your pruning is more in the order of 'trimming'. If you remove too much, you won't get the flowers.

Overgrown and neglected Group B clematis can be cut right down in the spring, but you will lose the best crop of flowers that year.

By way of encouragement, I can tell you that I cut back to ground level a very old Group B clematis completely one November. The next year it grew back and gave me a dozen or so flowers in mid- to late summer. The following spring it was absolutely, utterly wonderful. I now have to start thinning out the shoots that have flowered and doing all sorts of text-book stuff. Oh dear.

Group C (or 3) These really are the most useful and accommodating of them all. They are the ones I urge all those who have had zero luck with clematis so far to rush out and buy.

They flower abundantly from July to October on the shoots they make in the current season. There are loads to chose from, some of them really common like 'Jackmanii' (masses of deep-purple floppy flowers), and 'Perle d'Azur' (ethereal mauve/blue). There is a whole mob of smaller-flowered ones called 'viticella' clematis that grow and flower incredibly well and have a resistance to wilt, and there are some really wonderful later summer–autumn ones like *C. orientalis* (yellow), *C. flammula* and *C. rehderiana* (cream and scented) that give the garden a real lift when things are looking a bit dried out and drained of vigour.

How do you prune them? Oh joy, oh joy, it is simplicity itself. You can cut them to about knee-height in late February or March. If you are growing them up trees, you can cut them back to the branch level of their hosts whence they will scramble aloft again during the summer. All of this means that you can grow them into a variety of shrubs and roses and just prune them out once a year. No more bird's-nests.

You can actually cut them down at any time during the dormant months as long as the weather is not too frosty. When it's *that* cold I prefer to slum in to Tunbridge Wells and look at clothes shops. No danger of untimely clematis pruning round here, I assure you.

To sum up. Hurrah for Group C clematis.

Good Companions

Here are some **winning combinations** of climbers that work together with each other and with wall shrubs:

Rosa 'Mermaid' (pale yellow climbing rose) and *Clematis* 'Jackmanii Superba' (purple)

Rhamnus alaternus 'Argenteomarginata' (green and white variegated evergreen shrub, with tiny reddish buds) and *Clematis viticella* 'Kermesina' (deep red)

Rosa glauca (grey/purple-leaved shrub rose, with scarlet hips) and *Clematis* 'Madame Julia Correvon' (pink/scarlet)

Rosa 'Compassion' (apricot/pink climbing rose, with gold centre) and *Lonicera x heckrotii* 'Gold Flame' (apricot and goldish yellow honeysuckle)

Solanum crispum 'Glasnevin' (mauve/blue, with deep yellow centre) and yellow climbing nasturtiums

Clematis 'Perle d'Azur' (ethereal mauve/blue) and *Vitis vinifera* 'Purpurea' (purple-leaved ornamental vine)

Any shrub or climbing rose with *Clematis viticella* 'Alba Luxurians'

Cotinus coggygria 'Royal Purple' (plum foliage) and *Clematis* 'Nelly Moser' (mauve/pink)

Vitis coignetiae 'Claret Cloak' (reddish-leaved vine) with *Clematis viticella* 'Madame Julia Correvon' (pink/scarlet)

Early and late Dutch honeysuckle (*Lonicera periclymenum* 'Belgica' and *L. serotina*) grown together.

Lonicera periclymenum 'Graham Thomas' (cream-yellow honeysuckle) with *Clematis* 'Perle d'Azur' (ethereal mauve/blue)

CHAPTER 5

A Few Thoughts on Mixed Borders

have always found the words 'mixed border' quite intimidating, and I find myself using a Lady Bracknell voice just thinking them. It has to be said that most of us don't have 'mixed borders' in the proper sense. What many of us settle for can best be described as a 'mixed strip', generally along one or more sides of our gardens, where favoured plants alternately flourish, fail, flop over or run amok. Invariably, there are parts of these borders that are embarrassingly gappy at important times of year as well as in the winter, of course, and the whole thing is never, ever, quite satisfactory.

Perhaps, you might argue, I should spend my time and effort persuading people to try something new, something a little more 'now' than an old-fashioned mixed border. How about tropical gardens, perhaps, or gravel gardens? How about a bit of a dabble with the much vaunted 'new perennial planting'? Or should I give up completely and delve in depth into the delights of the dreaded decking?

I won't, however, because I really think that most garden fashions come and go. By the same token that most people (especially men) think that a lawn is an important and essential part of their gardens, most people (especially women) hanker after an area of harmonious planting in which to nurture and tend the plants they love, in other words a mixed border of some kind. We may play around with gravel and spiky plants, bog gardens or wild-flower patches here and there, but the need for a decent 'mixed border' has been planted deeply in the British gardening psyche. It is what this nation of gardeners is apparently admired for, so most of us just keep on fiddling away, trying to get it right.

First of all, what is a real mixed border: what exactly is it that we hanker after? The mixed border is the natural successor to the herbaceous borders of the gardening era when labour was cheap, gardens were large and it was acceptable for the wealthy to show off. Truly herbaceous borders – those composed entirely of plants that die right back in the winter – are few and far between these days. I remember as a small child (brought up with a tiny garden that was then home to rabbits and bantam hens, but with a large allotment) being amazed at a display of towering delphiniums in a huge old-fashioned herbaceous border at Bristol Zoo. To a six-year-old, they seemed taller and more magnificent than the elephants I had been taken to see, and I suppose that was the point of them: size and splendour, if only for a few short weeks of the year. We tend to demand more, and less, of our smaller gardens now. For a start, we want to look at something for the whole year, not just high summer. And most of us baulk at all the hard work that growing so much herbaceous stuff involves.

So the mixed border, in its proper form, is quite unashamedly a bit of this and a bit of that. It is a mixture of roses, flowering and foliage shrubs, both evergreen and deciduous, to give it some kind of permanent backbone. In among these are bulbs, biennials, a fair number of herbaceous perennials, and a few annuals thrown in for good measure (to fill up the gaps or add a bit of seasonal oomph). As the word border implies, the whole thing is set against a backdrop of a hedge, a fence or a wall, most probably with climbing plants on it as well. The real skill is sorting everything out so that it is relatively easy to service and maintain, and that things happen all over the place for as much of the year as possible. Alas, it takes time, patience and a lot of plant knowledge to get it really right.

There are wonderful examples of mixed borders in most of the major gardens in Britain, but these grand borders with their huge depth and enormous swaths of colour can seem all too daunting and irrelevant to the owners of small gardens. Indeed, you can well be put off the whole thing for ever as you realize, for example, that the amount of ground covered by pink phlox alone in Christopher Lloyd's famous Long Border at Great Dixter is just about equal to the entire square footage of your own (so-called) mixed border. Purists will tell you that you just can't do it on a small scale and that small borders look 'spotty' (a favourite put-down of the horticulturally challenged by the spatially privileged). However, in my view it is part of the on-going challenge that is real gardening: the annual keeping-the-fingers-crossed cliff-hanger to see if this year's wheezes work the way you want them to.

It is undoubtedly true that achieving a half-way decent patch of garden that you can call a mixed border without blushing is extremely hard in a small space and it takes time (a couple of years at the very least) to look established. If and when you do get it 'right', you will probably have changed your taste or gardening style and discovered a whole new lot of plants you simply must have. So the whole enterprise has to be seen as a constantly moving feast, a never-ending game. It is not for those seeking an easy gardening life. Even I have to admit that it is actually advisable for the owners of small borders to give up gardening altogether in the deepest, dreariest winter months. This is the time of year when owners of large borders bore the pants off you with tales of hoar frost on their herbaceous perennials or the ravishing red stems of their three square yards of cornus caught magically in the slanting winter sunlight. 'Small borderers' miss out on all that for obvious reasons, and anyway it sometimes gets too cold on February mornings to venture outside for the customary recce *en chemise de nuit*. It is far more fun at this time of year to spend any designated gardening time sitting in your socks leafing through bulb catalogues and old gardening magazines to give your fantasies a run for their money.

Where do you start?

I will approach borders from two directions. First, how do you tart up an old and boring one that doesn't work for you, and second, how do you make a new one out of virgin ground? In both cases the first move involves winning a battle for extra space, since I assume that as a gardening obsessive you are angling for a bigger slice of the garden pie in which to spread your horticultural wings (how about that for mixing three leisure-oriented metaphors?) This generally involves either pinching a bit of treasured lawn from a grassaholic, or banishing footballs, or confining children's ghastly plastic play rubbish to an invisible area under a dripping lime tree where nothing grows. None of these feats is easily achieved, as we all know.

I should say at this point that this book deliberately does not set out to give definite design advice. I am a dedicated graduate of the well-known sticks-and-string school of garden design, preferring to let gardens develop around my passion for plants rather than spend my time trying to tone down what can so easily become a runaway fantasy in bricks, paving and sawn timber (which often happens if you start using graph paper). I realize that I am extremely fortunate in that I have always been able to visualize what I want a garden to look like and, over time, have learned how to achieve the 'look' by teaching myself what works where in the garden. I have taken a lot of stick from professional garden designers, many of whom provide a missing link for their clients, mapping out for them a new shape for their garden that they cannot themselves 'see'. But, should you employ a designer, try to make sure that they do not stuff your garden full of plants that are, essentially, their choice. If you are at all interested in growing things, the real gardening begins once the designers and builders have left, as you personalize your garden and make it a place where you can fiddle around, make a few mistakes, but above all enjoy the plants that really please you. You need to understand what goes on out there, or your investment in the design can become a source of stress and anxiety which is absolutely what gardening should not be.

Old borders

First, size? Most of the 'wannabe' borders I have seen are just too small and mean to deserve the name. To get anything like a satisfying depth of planting, they need to be at the very least 1.5m deep at some point and about 2.5m long. This may seem unrealistically ambitious for a small garden, but can often be achieved by taking the planting area across one or more corners. Most of our gardens are square or rectangular, and such borders that exist are frequently just strips along the edges. By extending the planting area boldly across a corner, you not only achieve a greater depth, you distract the eye from the real shape of the garden which instantly adds interest.

Second, site? Logically, it makes sense to have your main border set away from the house, where you can see it from a good vantage point, usually from the kitchen sink, but, if you are lucky, from your living room window or terrace. Having decided on the best amendment to the shape of the border, you then have to consider which way it faces because you need to work out how much light it will get and for how many months of the year. It is really important that you take this into consideration since it affects what plants will be happy there. If the best site for your border happens to be in a north-facing corner, for example, don't despair. Happy well-grown shade-loving plants look splendid: you can go for big bold shiny leaves and ferns, for example, enlivened by variegated evergreens and a few tall white-flowered plants such as Japanese anemones, foxgloves or tobacco plants. The secret is to plant things that will grow well, rather than to hammer away with plants that need more light than you can provide, and that will never perform satisfactorily without it. I have explained more about the different types of light and shade in the chapter on shrubs (see pages 36-8), and these guidelines apply to all plants, not just shrubs.

Third, timing? The accepted time to do major things to your border is either October/November or about March. However, I find that if you get really fed up with your garden, a good time to start blitzing it is September. Most gardens are a bit shot by then. Our memory of what looked good and what looked awful is fresh, the weather is pleasant enough to work, children are back at school or wherever, and energy levels generally are high. You can still get herbaceous perennials at most garden centres and nurseries, some still with flowers on that will help you with your border planning. Furthermore, if you manage to get new things planted and old things replanted at this time, they may have a month or so to establish themselves in their new sites before the soil and the weather cool down. You may have to take a little extra care, making sure that the plants are watered in well, but in my view the benefits more than compensate for the extra work needed.

Existing plants? Once you accept the limitations of the aspect of your potential revamped border, you then have to take a good, long and, if necessary, ruthless look at the plants already growing in the area, to see if they fit into the new scheme of things. The most common problem I encounter is that even knowledgeable and otherwise sensible gardeners will hang on to plants, particularly roses and huge clumps of non-flowering irises or peonies just because they are there. On countless occasions, I have been asked to help reorganize a border and been told by the owner, in a tired and exasperated voice, that the stringy rose at the back just happened to get left there because when they moved in to the house it was the only plant in the entire garden that was in flower and that they recognized. The joke is that I have done this myself. I left a rich crimson rose in a key position in a softly coloured border in my old garden in Wandsworth. I started off by apologising for its presence in my otherwise tasteful border – it fortunately only had two major flushes of flower each season and I could hardly deadhead it soon enough. In the end, as the fashion for bolder colour schemes began to take hold, people started to tell me what a wonderful eye-catching statement the rose made. I nodded sagely every time (tongue firmly in cheek), shamelessly letting people believe that the rose was there intentionally. I quickly planted some purple delphiniums close by to enhance the 'feature'. So although, quite by chance, I got away with it, most of us don't, usually because the rose or whatever it is, gets unhealthy and fails to perform on any level through lack of care, and increasingly sticks out like a sore thumb. The moral of this story is that in most cases you should be much braver and remove anything that does not fit with your basic ideas. If you are really feeble you can give it away or (and this can either prolong the agony or occasionally give you a rich reward) move the culprit to a more suitable site in your own garden.

Large, immovable shrubs that you *definitely* want to keep and that are in *absolutely* the right place can be left in situ. You can build your new border around them, but you should think twice about keeping late-flowering whoppers like *Buddleia davidii* or lavatera in a small mixed border. They need such drastic pruning each spring to keep them in bounds that their presence makes it difficult to keep the border looking balanced, and obviously limits the number of other plants that will cope with the lack of elbow-room in the border in late summer.

Other plants, including herbaceous perennials, some biennial seedlings (foxgloves, honesty, forget-me-nots and so on) and whatever bulbs you unearth should be removed completely and re-sited temporarily in another part of the garden designated a 'nursery bed.' You should put labels with each clump, even with rough descriptions of the plants as you remember them since, although this decampment is only relatively short-term, it is amazing how quickly you forget what things are.

If your garden upheaval is not very large, there is no point in going to the trouble of creating a proper nursery bed. You can get away with spreading a sheet of plastic on the lawn or terrace, dumping on it the plants that you want to keep (with labels), covering all the roots with newspaper and wetting the whole area with a hose. As long as the plant roots are not exposed to sun and wind, and the newspaper remains moist, they should survive for a week or so.

Transplanting shrubs

As often as not there will be shrubs you want to keep that are definitely in the wrong place, and it really is worth having a go at transplanting them. Roses hate to be disturbed when they are in leaf or flower, and may just drop everything or even die if you try moving them. They will occasionally recover but, if you love them, it is not worth taking the risk. It might be better to wait until they are virtually leafless in November before undertaking the work in the border. Remember, shrubs, even person-sized ones, can be moved if it is really unavoidable. Some of them absolutely loathe root disturbance of any kind, and will let you know by wilting alarmingly for weeks. Worse, they may give up the ghost. Notable sulkers are hebes and most evergreens (try to move them during dull and windless weather), while large shrubby euphorbias and mature cistus behave even worse. But it is always worth having a go at transplanting things since it is better to have a stab at it than to chuck them out without a fight. Like a lot of gardening, it is all common sense really, but then, time and time again, common sense deserts obsessives. Guidelines for moving shrubs are included in the earlier chapter on shrubs (see pages 43-4).

Improving the soil

Once you have cleared out all the plants you want to reinstate in the new improved border, isolated the shrubs and roses you want to keep where they are and moved or thrown out the others, you can start to improve the soil with organic matter. There is more information about the necessity for this in the earlier chapter on soil (see pages 19-33).

I do recommend that you don't skimp on the amount of chunky organic stuff that you add to the soil before you plant up your border, be it well-rotted horse manure, mushroom compost, home-made compost, composted bark or some such 'soil improver'. Organic stuff plumps up and improves all soils, whether it is thick and clay-like or light and sandy, or something in between. Your plants will get a really good start and you will not need to think about adding any more, except as a mulch perhaps, for a year or even two. As a rough guide, you should reckon on digging in at least a bucketful, preferably two, of stuff plus, if you like, a roughly sprinkled handful of bonemeal or other phosphate per bucket into each square metre. Your plant roots will really appreciate it. If your soil is really ropey use more. At the same time as forking the stuff in, you will have the chance to weed properly, removing any spaghetti-like roots that are the hallmarks of troublesome perennial invasive customers such as bindweed and ground elder, and trying to get out whole the deep tap-roots of dandelions. By digging, you are bound to bring a lot of dormant weed seeds to the surface of the soil so you should not be deceived by the fact that you appear to have done a thorough job. You won't have, with just one go at it, but that shouldn't stop you trying, particularly with the aforementioned nasties.

Once you have done all this preparation, you can really start on the interesting bit – planning things out and shopping. But first I should, as I explained, approach border preparation from the other direction.

Completely new borders in virgin ground

As I have already said, new borders are generally created after often tricky negotiations with other interested parties about priorities in the garden. Be tough. It may be worth pointing out that there is no point in trying to have anything other than a row of sad and battered-looking climbers in a mean strip a couple of feet wide grudgingly sliced off the side of a football pitch.

Removing turf and then digging it into the soil before you plant so that it rots down underneath everything is an excellent way to make sure a new border is well fed. If you are making a border in a patch of former lawn, therefore, you should remove the grass in strips cutting it first into rectangles that you can slip your spade under – a bit like carving up flapjacks in a tin. This is a back-breaking job, made even harder if you are, like me in my new garden, daft enough to and try to remove what felt at the time like the entire surface of the globe on a very hot day when the lawn was rock hard and parched. It helps a lot, I subsequently found out, if you wait until the ground is moist and if you can borrow a special long-handled flat-bladed spade called a turfing iron. If you can't get hold of one of these, just soldier on with an ordinary spade, but take it slowly. Aim to take off a layer about 2in deep of the grass and as much of its roots as possible. If the grass is in good nick and not too full of weeds, save the best bits for patching other bald areas or the collapsed edges of the lawn. You will get better at removing the turf in a more orderly and regular way as you progress, so it makes sense (if you do want to save some for patching) to start with the worst area of grass first. Stack all the bits somewhere close by, because you will be digging them back in upside down shortly.

Trench digging

This is such a worthwhile thing to do before planting up a new border. It is a nightmare job it is true, but one which you can boast about for years as you watch your plants flourish. Basically what you do is divide your area into rectangles in your mind's eye, and tackle each rectangle of ground in turn. Starting, as it were, at the top right-hand corner of a rectangle, dig a trench across it at least a spade's depth deep, putting the soil you remove on a plastic sheet or in a barrow that you can drag or wheel to the other end of the plot. To dig efficiently and get a good rhythm going in what will inevitably be fairly compacted soil, jab your spade downwards vertically at right angles to your cutting line before removing each spadeful so that each clod comes out in a manageable squarish chunk. Then you place strips of old turf face down in the bottom of the trench and sprinkle a handful of bonemeal or general fertilizer for each linear yard of trench on top of the turf. Then you go back to the beginning of the row, step backwards and dig another trench, turning the contents over as you dump it on top of the upside-down turf in the first trench. Chop away at the soil to break up the clods. As you do this you may well see bits of dandelion root or bits of perennial weeds that got left behind during the turf-cutting operation, and these should be removed in case they sprout later. By putting the turf in upside down, you are minimizing the risk of it coming back up through your borders, but you should make sure that your trenches are deep enough not to let the grass get any silly ideas.

Work over the entire border area, finally putting the contents of the first trench you dug on top of the turf and fertilizer in the last trench that you dug. If you run out of turf (these things never work out the way they say in books) put a 4in layer of mushroom compost, rotted horse manure or any other organic stuff you can find in the bottom of the trenches.

Every so often, put your spade down, straighten up your spine, put your hands flat in the small of your back and gently stretch backwards, then roll your shoulders around. It all helps ease the strain.

At the end of the process you can stand back and feel so, *so* pleased with yourself. Then go and have a hot, smug bath.

Of course, not everyone has the time, the strength or the inclination to trench dig their gardens, and it really is not the end of the world if you don't. Furthermore, you will always find the odd (generally organic) gardener who says that so much disturbance to the soil is actually a bad thing. So if, for whatever reason, it suits you better not to go the whole hog, then you can just dump as much organic stuff as you can muster in an even layer over the soil and fork it in as deeply as you can, removing any weeds as you go, at the same time adding, if you feel inclined, a sprinkling of Growmore or chicken manure. You, too, will qualify for the deep, hot, smug bath after this.

Whatever you do in the way of digging, try to leave the area to settle down – give the worms time to calm down before you start to plant.

Planning a border

This is, quite frankly, one of the bits of this book that I have dreaded writing and, when I teach, it is the bit I dread teaching. I don't know how anyone ever constructively advises others on how to plant up a border since I am sure everyone just fiddles about in their own way and finally gets there, or doesn't. All I can offer are bits of rather mundane-sounding practical advice, when what people really want to get from you is a magic formula, a foolproof verbal planting plan.

The best description I ever read about how to go about border planting was written years ago by Christopher Lloyd. Presumably it struck a chord because it was so close to what I have tried to do, and explain, in the past. It was reassuring to find that he doesn't, or didn't then, mention drawing things out precisely to scale with perfect little coloured circles to indicate different plants, all in a meticulous, organized, tablets-of-stone sort of way. So it is without shame that I shall, with personal additions, subtractions and amendments, try to recall the gist of what he advised.

It is best if you make lists and then do some sort of blobby bird's eye view drawing before you even think of going shopping, and before you plant or replant a single thing. First, of all, list all of the plants you simply must have. This list will have on it things you have fallen for in other people's gardens, things you remember from childhood, things you couldn't imagine living without. To this list, add the plants that you already have, know and understand and that you really want to keep (these are the ones under the wet newspaper, remember?) When making your lists you must consider the growing requirements of the plants you want; I am sure I have gone on enough about sun, shade, moisture and general soil conditions and so on for you to realise that these things are of vital importance. Look plants up in books and generally familiarize yourself with them so that you know roughly how they can be expected to perform, and steadfastly root out any from your list that you know in your heart of hearts won't work properly.

I would add at this point that in my experience one should be very, very careful about being offered a load of dross by well-meaning and sympathetic friends, who, on seeing all that naked soil will, at the drop of a hat, treat your garden like a horticultural land-fill site, dumping on you all the overgrown and unruly hooligans from their own overstuffed borders. These are probably plants, incidentally, that they themselves unwittingly accepted in the same circumstances years earlier. So keep quiet about your new border, or you will find endless 'gifts' of *Chrysanthemum maximum*, anonymous watery orange oriental poppies and alstroemerias. *Sisyrinchium striatum* (the green-leaved self-seeder), yellow loosestrife, *Geranium* 'Claridge Druce', lemon balm and numerous others lovingly pressed in to your eager soily hands. (You may notice that *Geranium* 'Claridge Druce' is included in my Plant Lists on pages 156–7, however I recommend you use this plant purely as a temporary filler.) Each plant is pleasant enough in its way and in the right context (actually, I think I may be lying here), but none is the sort of unruly guest you want at your party, if you know what I mean. By all means beg and wheedle shamelessly for things you really want – that is what we all do. But remember you are in charge. Not your mother-in-law, not your best gardening friend, not your next door neighbour – not anyone. This is your baby. You haven't a hope in hell of getting things right for yourself if you go all weak at the knees and are grateful for any old cast-offs.

Back to the border. First, the nuts and bolts bit. Get your back-row of climbers sorted out, making sure before you plant them that they will have adequate support – or they will yawn forward on to all your other new plants. Remember that if you have a hedge or plants that need mid-season pruning and tweaking, you need to be able to get to them somehow. If you have a decent depth to the border, make a path – it need only be a narrow strip with bark chippings on it or some stepping stones – from which to service the back of it. It may seem like a waste of precious planting space, but you will regret it if you don't put it in at the start, and it will soon be virtually hidden as things grow so that only you will know where you can tread. In my former gardens I ignored this important piece of advice that I used to hand out with such aplomb (do as I say, not as I do). I seemed to spend my life during the summer teetering painfully on one cramped leg trying not to snap the delphiniums off while I wrestled with the climbers from next door that were trying to muscle in on the act, as I tried to twist my body so I could dead-head all around me. Daft. I am much more grown up now, I hasten to say. Paths simply everywhere and climbers properly catered for.

Some borders – especially in small gardens where you are often trying to distract the eye from a less than lovely view of the neighbouring buildings – look good if they contain a big show-off plant. Current fashion may well steer you towards a spiky thing – a phormium, perhaps, or, if your garden is sheltered, a cordyline. Or it could be a bit of rounded or pointed evergreen blobbery, like a bit of clipped box, or something that isn't a plant at all, like a sundial or an urn. Whatever it is, it will provide you with a your foundation stone, from which you build your border outwards.

Next turn your attention to any shrubs you want to include. I think they look better in a harmonizing group of two or three if there is space. Ideally, each member of the group should do its thing at a different time of the year, or have a strong contrast in leaf shape or colour with its neighbour. Don't forget about the bleak winter months completely; make sure that you include evergreens, preferably ones that also flower well. When it comes to deciding where they should be placed in the border, don't, however, plant them where they will block the view of the rest of your border from your best vantage point. Or where they will steal the thunder, as it were, from any deliberately eye-catching feature described above.

If you simply must have roses in your border, remember you cannot plant a new rose in the place of an old one without changing the soil. Also, remember that gorgeous old shrub roses are quite hard to accommodate in smaller borders because they flower for such a short time and have such wide-spreading shapes. Look instead at some of the hybrid perpetual or modern shrub roses which flower for longer and some of which (such as 'Ballerina') are smaller or work well as standards at the back of the border to give height.

I could go on – with various platitudinous utterings about autumn leaf colour, shrubs with berries or coloured stems for winter – but it is exactly the sort of smug stuff in gardening books that I have always found so irritating. What you want is chapter and verse, and all I would be giving you is the address of the library! Just remember, it is your taste, not mine or anyone else's, that is important. All I can do is help you to think in the right way, but I will give you an example or two of shrub groups in borders that have worked for me in the past:

Evergreens for backbone and a rounded shape: *Choisya ternata* with *Pittosporum* 'Irene Paterson'.
Tall evergreens to hide a fence (limited sun): *Viburnum tinus* and *Rhamnus alaternus*'Argenteomarginata' with late-flowering *Clematis viticella* 'Kermesina' struggling through both.
Evergreen flowering shrubs for hot sunny site: *Phlomis fruticosa* and *Cistus purpureus* (with very tall deciduous *Cytisus battandieri* and *Berberis thunbergii* and a semi-evergreen weeping bamboo, *Fargesia murieliae*, behind, making in all a thick, deep, fence-hiding bank of shrubs).

Once you have decided on all this, you ought to try to do your blobby drawing on a large sheet of paper. It doesn't have to be done to scale but you should try to make the proportions of the bed look about right, and have a rough idea of the actual length and depth of the new border by pacing it out (a large female stride equals about a metre). Start with your 'foundation stone' plant and find something from your list that would look good with it. Draw little cloud-shaped dollops on the page for each plant and put the name in each. Individual things like fox gloves that you may well want to plant in groups you can mark with crosses. Tick things off from your list as you go, and gradually build outwards in all directions, thinking all the time how things would look with their intended neighbours. Incorporate some of the 'must have' combinations of plants that you will doubtless have filed away in your brain as a result of ogling other people's borders. If your border is not going to have a focal point as such, start at one corner or a prominent place with a fairly large patch of something eye-catching, and work your way outwards from there.

Plan to leave plenty of space around shrubs; they are going to grow like the wind because of the enriched soil. Aim to put annuals next to them, or even biennials or bulbs, but don't make them fight it out with precious young perennials. The shrubs will probably win and you will have wasted time and money.

If the budget will allow and there is sufficient space, do plan to plant groups of things rather than single plants. All that advice that you simply must plant in threes, fives or sevens with about 2ft of space between each item is a bit hard to take when you have a small garden and there are so many things you want to try out. But while you can plant bigger things like acanthus as a single plant (and it will make a decent sized statement from the start), the smaller perennials will get lost in singles. You could always do what I do – it works in the short term: plant two of the same thing quite close together to make a bigger single clump that you can then divide after a year. Do a swap with a friend or heave something else out of the border that doesn't work in order to create more space. I did warn you that this border thing was a movable feast.

All the time you are 'weaving' your tapestry on paper and ticking things off your lists, think about not only what goes well with what, but consider what happens to each plant and when, so that you don't get all the action going on in only one part of the border at a time. There is a lot to think about, so my advice is that the *last* thing you should think about is colour. Unless you are blessed with a superhuman colour sense, this is the straw that can break the camel's back and get you completely bogged down. I have always maintained that colour is the last thing you should try to get right, and not the first, since this is where a lot of people go wrong. At the end of the day, plants are part of nature, and nature rarely jars the colour senses. I think you need to get your plants up and running – growing well – and once you are confident about them you can start reshuffling the pack, as it were, to get the colours right for you. That is how I learned, anyway.

I will, however, say one or two things on the subject of colour, that may be helpful. While I think that colour-themed borders are a bit of a cop out, there is much to be said for the addition of white in a new, otherwise colour-chaotic border. It separates things out and calms things down. I have already extolled the virtues of white foxgloves and white Japanese anemones and others, but there is a white-flowered lime-green leaved plant that I find immensely useful in a new border to give a nice pillowy over-all look, and that is golden-leafed feverfew. And even if it self-seeds in a rather thuggish way – plenty of gardeners think of it as a weed – you can recognize the seedlings at a glance, since they are so bright, and get rid of them. Another similar self-seeding thug/god-send for a young border is the lofty plum-leaved red orach. I rather like having these two as more or less permanent, but easily controllable members of my garden mafia. It means that there need never be any major gaps. This is hardly what you call sophisticated gardening, but there you go.

Shopping and Planting — At Last

Hopefully, you will find most of the plants you want at local garden centres and nurseries. Use the phone; also use that wonderful publication, *The RHS Plant Finder*, which will tell you who sells what all over the country. Again, use the phone as it is very disheartening to drive 30 miles for a plant that isn't there.

Whatever you do, don't start planting until you have at least three-quarters of the things you want to plant. For the ones you can't get hold of, you will have to make up sticks that are approximately the appropriate height, with labels on them. 'Plant' these sticks as reminders until such time as you can get the plants themselves. As a last resort, you may have to find substitutes.

First consult your 'plan', and place your plants, still in their pots, where you intend them to go. Don't move your plants or transplant from under the newspaper till the last possible moment – there is probably still quite a lot of shuffling things around to do and they won't like the wait. Do try your very best not to plant things too close together in the mistaken hope that the border will establish itself more quickly the more plants you put in. Remember that new borders *always* look naked and awful, if they are properly planted. If you get desperate, you can always add a few annuals in the first growing season – although you should watch out in case they get too big in the rich soil you have created and start cramping the style of the permanent plants.

If you have done your homework, you will have a fair idea about (eventual) relative sizes of plants, but don't be too boring about it. A few taller, slim or wafty plants towards the front of the border add a bit of oomph and stop the planting looking unnatural. Although this is rather a sophisticated piece of advice to give a first-time mixed borderer, it is a useful concept to take on board. If all else fails, you can trot it out in the presence of bemused acquaintances to justify the mistakes that appear a few months down the line.

When you are reasonably sure of where things are going to go, plant them. Make sure that the roots of all the new plants are nice and damp. I generally soak them in a bucket of water with something like Phostrogen dissolved in it, just to give them a boost. If you have done your soil preparation properly you don't really need to add any more goodies to the soil. However, when the weather is very warm and the soil dry, water each plant into its hole before you earth it up and firm it down, but don't water thereafter for a week or so. It is worth remembering that the dry soil on the surface, surprisingly enough, holds in the moisture down below. This is why experienced gardeners never fiddle with the soil surface during a drought – it makes matters worse.

If you are both dedicated and energetic, you could apply an organic mulch of composted bark, or similar, over the entire border. I don't like using coarse bark chippings as a general mulch as the blackbirds play very messy games of football with it on the lawn. To be effective (that is, to smother emerging weeds and retain moisture properly) a mulch has to be at least 3in thick, which means you need an awful lot of organic stuff. The downside to applying an all-over mulch – in addition to the sheer amount of hard work involved – is that if you do want to change the planting or move anything around, you have to scrape it all away and you end up 'losing' it.

Now what?

You are unlikely to have got things right first time. Some things will work, others won't, and some things will take a lot longer to establish themselves than others and you will change your mind about what you are trying to achieve anyway. You can make minor adjustments before the first growing season really kicks in, but then stop and let things develop for a while. You should try to resist the temptation to play chess with your new plants all the time. I know plenty of keen-as-mustard gardeners who are absolutely hopeless in this department and nothing ever gets going. However, there are three things that simply must be addressed even in the first growing season of a new border, the first two of which very rarely are: staking, deadheading and watering.

Staking

When you look at a 'grand' border in full sail in June and July, you can't really see all the hard work that went into it as little as a month earlier. The plants just stand there in all their glory. Underneath, holding it all erect so that gusts of wind or thunderstorms make little impression on it, is an absolute mass of stuff. The whole border is usually wearing the equivalent of a whalebone corset. Next time you look at a grand border put your hand in among the foliage, and you will feel it. It is all very ingenious.

The best way of supporting all sorts of herbaceous plants – the soft-stemmed ones that need the corsets – is undoubtedly to stick twigs (generally called 'pea sticks') around the individual clumps as they grow, so that they actually come up through them and are supported virtually invisibly by them for the whole season. Some gardeners weave hazel and willow into wondrous structures that are works of art in themselves. If you visit a grand garden border in May you can see how it is all done. In towns, it is hard to get hold of such things as hazel twigs in great quantities, so you have to resort to other methods, the easiest of which is to use traditional bamboo canes and garden twine. You should insert at least four canes around each plant clump, tying one end of a piece of twine to one cane using a clove hitch, then looping it around the other canes in the group and across the circle to and fro if it is a big plant, before tying the two ends of twine together to make a firm web-like support through which the plant can grow.

Plants, such as delphiniums, that grow with heavy spires of flowers should have a cane inserted for each flower spike, and they should then be tied laboriously to the cane as they grow. If you use the cane and web of string method, the heavy head of the flower spike invariably breaks off in a rainstorm in the middle of June.

You soon get the hang of staking plants by trial and error. Paeonies, for example, need expensive wire mesh supports to hold their heads up for the few days that they flower – yet another reason not to grow paeonies, with which so many people are so irrationally besotted. Not many people go to the trouble of supporting herbaceous geraniums ('Johnson's Blue', 'Wargrave Pink', 'Mrs. Kendall Clark' and others) but they look a million dollars if you do, and even pansies appreciate a leg up and may well sprawl on upwards into neighbours in a very acceptable way.

Should you develop a passion for plants of grand operatic proportions, it doesn't necessarily mean that you have to also go into the scaffolding business. That Pavarotti amongst perennials, the giant thistle-like cardoon, seems to hang in there without support. If limbs happen to lean – probably because of less than full sunlight – amputation is probably the only solution. Divas such as *Acanthus mollis* need no support at all, nor do some of the larger ladies in the chorus such as *Phlox paniculata*, bless them. Penstemons and *Knautia macedonica* are like wild-eyed sopranos with big hair and will constantly escape from their supports and blowse charmingly all over the place for weeks whatever you do, so it is best not to bother. But a lot of the other big border players – the delphiniums we have already mentioned, and brittle things like *Galega officinalis*, *Salvia uliginosa* and *Cephalaria gigantea* as well as countless others, are not worth growing unless you make an effort to support them, especially if your garden is windy. As I say, you get the hang of it all in due course.

Whatever method suits you and your plants, the key is to get your supports in early, before the plants have grown too tall for you to get into the border without wreaking havoc. And tie them up loosely. Plants, like people, can't relax – and look utterly miserable – if their waistbands are too tight.

In the early days of your border, before you get to know who needs what by way of support, it might be as well to invest in a load of Y-stakes, curiously shaped bits of metal in various lengths, that are great for first aid, midsummer staking in new borders.

Deadheading

The reason that plants flower is to attract insects that pollinate them so that they can produce seeds, reproduce themselves and then, in the case of herbaceous plants, die back or die off completely. Once they have been pollinated and produced seeds, they stop flowering; the season's work is done. This is all very tedious for gardeners in summer, who want their plants to flower their socks off for as long a season as possible, while they deservedly sit back at last and enjoy the garden that has been their often exhausting obsession during the rest of the year. Deadheading is therefore the systematic removal of old, tired flowers almost before the plant realizes what is happening, in order to fool it into producing new ones. That is all there is to it really, except that, depending on the type of plant, you can make it look even uglier if you fail to remove a section of stalk (down to where you can see the next flower bud emerging) as you remove the flower head. Plants that are forced to work so hard in turn deserve extra feeding, and a foliar feed with one of the 'steroids for plants' variety, high in potash (Miraclegro or some such) gives great rewards. If you are not familiar with foliar feeding, now is the time to become so. Plants can actually feed through their leaves, so all you do is mix up the recommended dilution of one of these wonder feeds, or you can use a seaweed-based organic one if you prefer, and swish over the entire border with a watering can, preferably in the early morning or in the evening. A great pick-me-up for all.

Deadheading is a labour of love, best carried out in the evening, kitchen scissors in one hand, a glass of wine in the other, and with a big old flower pot or one of those expensive Sussex trugs nearby in which to throw any bits you manage to catch.

Equally, do it in the morning on your first pad round the garden. But is a satisfying thing to do as well, and for me it provides a time when I can actually listen to my lovely blackbirds, to the sound of our little fountain dripping into the pond, and breathe in all the wonderful gardeny, planty smells that are so powerful at the end of each day. And when I am doing something so comparatively effortless I can really enjoy the garden in a way that is utterly peaceful. It makes me forget all the mud, indecision and backaches so that I realize why I love gardening so much. Try it; you'll see.

By mid-July even in the mildest and greyest of British summers borders can run out of steam. Just as the grass slows down and goes beige, so, in their way, do the borders. All the early flowerers, such as the pansies and geraniums have gone stringy. Decapitated delphiniums and lupins are ragged and yellowing despite our best efforts. What the whole garden needs is a really good tidy up and cut back. If you do this now, removing old foliage and stumpy old flowers shoots by the barrow load, and if you can find the time and energy to then water, liquid feed, mulch and slug pellet everything at the same time, you can completely rejuvenate a border and kick start it into late summer activity. You need to be brave, and cut back much further than your instincts will allow. Cut pansies right back to the bone. Give the old tired shoots of geraniums a short, sharp tug and they will come completely away at the base, revealing the new foliage ready to put on a fresh performance. Take the shears to the catmint (give all the bits to your amazed and gratefully stoned cat), and cut all the old stems right out of the delphiniums. Of course, you will have to endure temporary gaps in the border here and there. But the whole process restores not only the garden's spirits, but also your own. It is thus a really worthwhile job to do. And if you are really organized and grown up about it, you will have some lilies or tobacco plants in big heavy pots waiting in the wings. Not to be planted, you understand, but to be stood with the blatant intent to deceive, in the 'holes' created by your late-in-the-day butchery in the border.

Watering

And so we come to watering, the bit people do generally less than efficiently. Presuming that you have planted up your border thoughtfully and done all the right things by your plants in the first instance, they should be able to get going in their first season without too much bother. Certainly a weekly check to make sure that they are not suffering in the hottest part of the summer should suffice.

When you do water, water precisely, aiming the watering can or hose low down so that you reach the plants' roots and don't waste time and water soaking the leaves. Put a rose on the end of the watering can, or use a hose with a rose end (I have an excellent lance-type hose end that reaches right into the back of the border). You should try to avoid anyone 'helpfully' applying violent jets of water to the soil/plants, which can make the border into a mud lake, and which in turn can damage the structure of the soil. And water *thoroughly*. A new plant needs to be encouraged to put its roots downward, eventually to find its own water. Too little a dose via a watering can or hose can be counterproductive, and only encourages surface rooting. In my new garden I have been quite tough and ruthless. I rarely water on the grounds that I am far too busy with other jobs to be a nursemaid to my plants. This hard-hearted attitude has led to generally good results, but it takes years to get out of the nurturing/molly-coddling frame of mind that seems to come all too naturally. As a rough rule of thumb, I would say that in a dry spell, a new, fast-growing shrub or perennial should have two gallons of water applied very slowly once a fortnight.

I am not a great fan of watering systems, but I have to admit that I've never had a 'pukka' one. I did resort to snaking a 'leaky hose' (the purpose-built porous pipe you can buy at garden centres) through the back of one of my London borders after a particularly arid summer but the next year it rained more, and I generally forgot to use it. The gardens I have seen that have proper watering systems all seem to change in character in a subtle way, not always for the better. Plants that previously coped without much water, luxuriating with frequently dampened feet, suddenly put on a spurt of lush growth and start to dominate the garden, while at the back of the crowd, someone often gets missed out and languishes quietly. At the other end of the spectrum, I have seen expensively installed watering systems that have been completely mishandled. They are often turned on each day for too short a time, so that their equally expensive all-over layer of mulch is barely dampened, and the plants remain none the wiser as to the trouble to which their owners have gone to ensure their survival.

I suppose watering systems that are properly installed and managed can save busy gardeners a lot of time, but by turning on the garden tap you can be lulled into missing out on the daily garden inspection which is so pleasurable and vital. I find that watering, or deadheading, or checking on the plant supports are all essential parts of the relaxation buzz.

Mixed Border Memorandum for the Year

Summer

1   Check plant stakes and supports regularly. Delphiniums may need a 5-ft high cane per spire, tied in every 6in, not a ring of wire or string, otherwise they topple.

2   Deadhead all the time, removing stalks as well as heads, but let biennials ripen some seeds before discarding them.

3   Thin out early-flowering shrubs, removing the shoots that have borne flowers and something larger from below, even if it means diving in to the back of the border.

4   If unwanted gaps appear in the border, fill them with plants (lilies, perhaps) in clay pots sunk in to the soil, but do not forget to water them.

5   Treat mildew on roses, asters, phlox and so on, with Tumbleblight or Nimrod-T.

6   Mulch and feed shrubs and roses in July, to give them a boost for the later summer. Continue foliar feeding the whole border, which will be 'tired' by July, using a high potash feed to promote flowering.

Autumn

1   Continue deadheading until the battle is lost. In a wet season, more generous cutting back in July/August can provoke a surprisingly lush second flush of colour.

2   In late October, if you can hold off that long, cut down perennials by half, throw away spent annuals, and take stock of what needs to be done in the way of dividing, transplanting and replacing perennials.

3   Mulch established plants with compost or well-rotted manure. Always plant or replant with compost and plenty of organic stuff. Do not apply fertilizers high in nitrogen at this time of year.

4   Label plants, or leave markers or supports in situ – most herbaceous perennials completely die down in the winter.

5   Tidy up shrubs; there should be no need to prune heavily. Remove top weight from roses and spray them with Nimrod-T or other fungicide.

6   Plant tulips, daffodils, alliums, always in groups, and with a marker.

7   Search the garden for young biennial seedlings – forget-me-nots, honesty, foxglove, and so forth to fill up any gaps.

Winter

1 Remove any late-autumn growth from perennials; cut down to about 4in.

2 Put down slug pellets, or water entire border with Liquid Sluggit – which gets to the small black slugs that actually live in the soil and eat roots. Also keep the border free of drifts of dead leaves which slugs and snails use as duvets.

3 Make sure that hardy fuchsias and any other tender perennials have a good dome of mulch over their bases – they will shoot earlier if protected from frost in this way.

4 Good lily bulbs become available in late winter. Do not buy them pre-packed. Go for fat, solid bulbs sold loose in boxes of peat. Plant them as soon as you get them if the ground is soft enough, 3in down, with plenty of leaf mould or compost, in groups of three or more. Put in markers or you will dig them up by mistake.

Spring

1 Look out for pests early on – slugs remain active throughout a mild winter. Whitefly smother wall shrubs, particularly honeysuckle (use Polysect) and aphids will attack early rose shoots (use Rapid).

2 Prune roses and late-flowering shrubs. Apply a mulch around their bases and give them all a rose food (e.g. Toprose) which is high in potash to induce good flowering.

3 Put plant stakes in place *early*, so that perennials can grow up through them.

4 Adjustments can be made in the border up to mid-April, but plant with even greater care and water well in hot weather.

5 If you did not apply much organic stuff to the rest of the border in the autumn do it now, together with a balanced fertilizer if you are so inclined. Take care not to damage emerging shoots. In late spring you can start foliar feeding with a soluble fertilizer, particularly if the weather is dry.

6 In late spring, plant out tobacco plants and other annuals. Do not be tempted to do this too early – there is no point – they will not get going until the soil warms up.

7 Cut back hardy fuchsias to the ground – even after a mild winter when they will shoot out from quite high up on their previous growth. They make much better plants if cut down, but will start to flower month or so later.

CHAPTER 6

Lawns – Ghastly Sparse Grass

We shall not linger long on lawns

I often go on about the great gardening divide: chaps look after the lawn and guard every inch of it with their lives, likewise hedges, fences and other man-the-hunter, 'Englishman's home is his castle' stuff, while girls like flowers and all the pretty bits. If you think about it, I am sure you will agree that, whether you like the idea or not, broadly speaking this is true. I do not know many women gardeners who are finicky about looking after the grass or boundary hedges, and I do not know many men who rule the roost in a mixed border or a gravel garden. Of course you do get the odd neat-and-tidy gardeners – the women who put their (clean) wellies away all the time, have weed-free borders and keep all their plant labels in a file in the kitchen drawer and off whose garden shed floors you could safely eat your dinner. These traitors to the cause will doggedly slave away at the lawn edges before the arrival of guests, even sweeping up the bits, because they do not want tatty edges to ruin the look of their otherwise spotless, perfect gardens. But, on the whole, women are happy enough if the lawn is just green for most of the time, and appreciate the fact that grass is easier on their children's knees than any of the more fashionable and labour-saving alternatives, such as paving, gravel or decking. And the really soppy ones actually like daisies on the lawn because it reminds them of their schooldays

A lawn, let it not be forgotten, is a closely packed collection of small herbaceous perennials that we walk on, jump up and down on, cut back hard once a week for half of the year and abandon for the other half. It is no wonder, therefore, that small gardens in particular have bad lawns. Grass plants, just like other plants, need air, light, water and food to survive, and in the 'average family garden' (whatever that is) we seem to make life very difficult for them. First, I will look in greater detail at what makes our lawns so dire and then, assuming (rather arrogantly) that you are true to your gender type and a bit of a lawn slacker, we will look at the minimum you can do to have a green lawn, and at which of the many boring lawn jobs are worth the effort. First what are the main causes of ghastly grass?

Bad drainage

This is an awful, generally invisible problem that afflicts many new gardens, or gardens that have been 'landscaped', and is particularly common in areas of clay soil. Unsuspecting owners can be totally unaware that builders may have slapped down a load of turf-like carpet tiles over compacted subsoil on which JCBs and their like have been shunting around for weeks. The result is, come the winter rain, the garden can turn into a duck pond and, needless to say, grass doesn't like this much.

Overuse

There are generally areas of every lawn – entrances and exits from terraces, and around play areas, for example – that take such a battering that the soil beneath becomes too compacted for grass roots to survive. As a result, coarser, tougher and much less demanding plants – weeds and moss – start to take over. Even worse, the soil becomes alternately baked or waterlogged, so nothing at all will grow. The result is that you get completely bald patches that fail to green up in the spring, when even the worst lawns look their best.

Not enough light

Large shrubs and trees in small spaces form a dense canopy for the later part of the year, so grass becomes thin. Again, moss and weeds tolerant of shade and drought infiltrate the area (most troublesome is creeping buttercup, which marches across shady lawns at an alarming rate, throwing out runners in every direction). The grass is squeezed out and eventually packs up.

Bad mowing

Grass is either tended by a fanatic who, heavily influenced by cricket pitches, golf courses or rose-tinted memories of those immaculate green swards of childhood, mows it to a crisp beige stubble every week. Or it suffers from haphazard occasional mowing by someone who doesn't give a fig, so once every so often the grass gets the shock of its life from which it takes ages to recover. Maybe, just maybe, I am exaggerating a bit, but I am sure you get the picture.

I should say at this point that it is not all the fault of rampant grassaholics. For many of us a garden is not a proper garden without grass. You should, however, consider the possibility of other surfaces if your garden is really, really small. Banish the words 'concrete' and 'jungle' from your mind – there are lots of ways of using paving, bricks and such like that will enhance a small garden in a way that an ailing patch of damp weedy grass will not. It can actually be a relief not to be constantly fussing over grass in a small hostile environment, and the garden can be usable for twelve months of the year and in most weather conditions. But if a lawn is what you absolutely have to have, then you should take on board the following and act on as much of the advice as you feel inclined to.

Drainage is a huge problem in some gardens. Quite apart from the lawn, numerous plants will turn up their toes as a result of bad drainage. As far grass is concerned, however, if the problem is localized and not too bad, you can, in the first instance, apply a sandy top dressing twice a year after removing plugs of turf with a hollow tine aerator (more of that later). What you should not do is re-turf annually, without addressing the cause of the problem at all. I have known people do this, and one has to draw the conclusion that they must have more money than sense. For the same outlay they could have employed someone to put in a proper drainage system and solved the problem once and for all.

As for the worn-out bits, think about strategically placed stepping stones on areas of unavoidable compaction. Set them very slightly below the level of the lawn so that you can mow straight over them without murdering the lawnmower. Be aware that people and animals have a knack of making paths for themselves to get from A to B. They will do this rather than using those provided for them, if they subconsciously decide that these take them from A to B via J or even W. By which I mean, have a look and see if your paths are in the right place, or whether by moving them, or doing a bit of transplanting or braver pruning, you would have a better-looking lawn and a more cheerful lawnkeeper.

You could be really radical and give up trying to grow grass around children's play equipment; it makes mowing difficult anyway. You could dedicate a small corner of the garden to all that dreadful plastic play stuff, keeping it on a bed of composted bark, edged with timber gravel boards. If you can't do this, you could adapt a neat trick I once saw: under a swing the owner of this garden had bedded a small piece of that rather nasty semi-rigid brown clematis support-mesh in the lawn. The presence of the mesh seemed to stop feet from scuffing the soil away, and helped the grass to survive. I expect ordinary dark green chicken wire would work just as well, and that you could also use the same method for protecting the grass at the end of a slide. You should, of course, make sure somehow that the corners are well anchored, so that they don't curl upwards and trip up small people.

If your grass starts off each spring looking reasonably chipper, but takes a bit of a nose-dive in late summer, and if you have creeping buttercup invading your lawn, shade is your problem. Take a critical look at your shrubs and any trees that hang over your garden. You can often thin out the canopies of overhanging trees, or even remove a few lower branches. This will have a surprisingly dramatic effect, letting in more light and rain. Or you can have them pruned hard every two or three years. The proximity of trees to your precious lawn means that inevitably the ground will be deeply dry. An annual top dressing with a mixture that is heavy on peat or something equally moisture-retentive will help the grass to survive.

Also in shadier gardens, if the shrubs overhang the grass looking for light you should not be so mean with the size of your borders. Properly cut-out beds with shade-tolerant ground-cover plants, spring bulbs, and so on look far better than sparse grass petering out into barren soil. Be realistic, how much usable 'lawn' will you have lost? A smart move is to put in a mowing strip – a defining edge of brick or paving – and not let the grass or the border plants trespass in to each other's territory.

While we are on the subject of defining edges, you can completely transform the look of a whole garden, whether it is shady or not, by giving your lawn an immaculate edge. It is not important whether you chose to go for broad sweeping curves (as opposed to indecisive nibbles in and out of unpruned shrubs), or dead-straight formal edges. If those edges are cleanly cut, with a little gully at the edge of the border that collects wind-blown debris and makes it easier to shear the edges, it will look as though someone knows what they are up to and has taken a bit of trouble, even if they don't and they haven't much.

Shade you can't manipulate – that which is cast by high walls or intransigent neighbour's trees, particularly conifers – can be a gardener's nightmare. The problem is compounded by extreme drought and acid soil that may be full of matted tree roots. This is another instance where it is not practical to keep on banging away at growing grass. You may just have to play around with the design of the garden so the no-go area can accommodate a shed, a climbing frame, a seating area or a beautiful pot with something in it.

Routine Chores To Benefit Even The Worst Lawns

Mowing

Lawns under stress should *not* be mown too short. The turf of an ordinary garden is not the same as that of a golf course or bowling green. It consists of coarser and harder-wearing grasses and is meant to be kept longer. If mown too frequently or too short, it will weaken. Furthermore, domestic lawns are never really flat because of the use they get, so short mowing will result in the scalping of the high bits, which in turn will lead to the dying off of grass and the arrival of moss. You should start mowing, with the mower set on a high setting, as soon as the grass gets active – in towns that could be as early as late February. Between late April and mid-July it all gets rather hectic, with everything building to a once-a-week crescendo around the beginning of June. You can drop the height of the blade on the mower, but not to its lowest setting. With mowing, little and often is the key, and if you leave it for too long between cuts and have to mow it when it is several inches high – which means it is probably damp as well – it can look frightful afterwards. Towards the end of the summer grass growth mercifully slows down so everything can be allowed to go a little beige. September rain causes a startling revival, and mowing at this end of the season, I find, is the most difficult to organize. In small airless, sheltered gardens you may need to mow almost up to Christmas, but the grass is rarely dry enough. The only advice I can give is that you should seize the opportunities as they arise, and never put mowing off till another day.

A word about mowers: grassaholics, desperate for the day when they can play at being groundsmen and get a sit-on mower, will doubtless insist on a cylinder mower with a roller so that they can practice making stripes just like their dad's. These mowers do not cope with wet grass very well, clog up and cause a lot of bad language. Rotary mowers (you can get them with little rollers on the back), while not giving the same finish, cope with the wet far better. Their acquisition is therefore to be encouraged, if not insisted upon.

Raking

This is the job that hardly anyone does but it is one that makes a huge difference. At the end of the summer, rake out the build-up of dead grass and general mossy thatch using a special lawn rake. You can be quite tough. In fact, it is quite alarming what comes out, and at first you are convinced that you are pulling up all the grass. But only the weak or dead grass plants come out, along with Lego men's hats, sweet wrappers, ring pulls, small plastic farm animals, mystery apricot stones and countless brightly coloured bouncy balls. Amazing really. Do it again (but more gently because the grass is a bit fragile) in the spring to 'raise the pile' as it were before your first mow.

Aerating

Dedicated lawnists will derive a lot of satisfaction from this, which is without doubt a really worthwhile, but mind-numbing, bit of drudgery.

If your overall drainage is bad, you will have to do a serious aeration job every other year in the spring or autumn, using a hollow-tine fork which actually removes little plugs of soil from the top three inches of the lawn. You can hire these gizmos from hire shops, or share one with a similarly afflicted and dedicated neighbour, if you have one. It is really hard to get the fork into a compacted lawn and should not be attempted by the truly feeble, or when the lawn is anything other than soaking. One year in my London garden (where the little lawn had to cope with upwards of 300 visitors tramping about on it in one afternoon each year) I resorted to aerating the lawn in the middle of a downpour. It seemed to work a treat, and the water almost made plughole noises as it drained away to the Australian desert. To make a really good job of it, you should then follow up with top dressing (see below), using a sandy mixture, which will help the drainage of the lawn considerably. Those with less of a problem and still less enthusiasm, who perhaps want to improve the drainage in a small area of the lawn that has become compacted, can use a garden fork. Even this is hard work, and I find the only way to do a decent job of getting the fork in deep enough is to throw it into the ground with all one's strength, then wiggle it around before pulling it out. Obviously the garden fork method does not do quite the same job as the hollow-tine fork, since you are not actually displacing any soil. But it is better than doing nothing at all.

Top dressing

This, particularly in conjunction with aerating described above, is *absolutely* the best thing you can do to a lawn, but should not be confused with fertilizing. Top dressing involves adding a very thin layer of a sandy-peaty soil to the lawn's surface. Some of it will find its way down the aeration holes, and will improve the drainage and condition of the lawn. Top dressing, also sold as 'turf dressing', can be bought in bags from a garden centre although in my experience not all of them sell it. It is generally a 50/50 mixture of sand and peat or peat substitute. You could mix your own, but I think it is simpler to buy it ready bagged and add more sand or more moisture-retentive stuff depending on what your lawn problem is.

To spread it, you dump a large spadeful of the mixture at intervals of one square yard all over your lawn, and then brush it in with a stiff yard-broom. Do it when the grass is dry and freshly mown. When you have finished, you will hardly notice that you have done anything at all, so thin is the layer you have applied, so this is clearly not a job for those who need lots of appreciation for all their hard work. Grassaholics will want to go further and even out the bumps and dips with top dressing, but this is not really sensible and you are more likely to obliterate the grass in the dips than improve the situation to any noticeable degree. If grassaholics have got it that bad, they should acquire a proper lawn book and mug up on how to peel back the turf, add soil beneath it and then put it back. Quite!

Feeding

There is no law that says you have to feed your lawn, and many gardeners find the 'rush of blood to the head' green-ness lawns take on after they have been fed in the spring intensely unattractive. But if you care enough, and want your grass to go dark green and lush, then give it a high-nitrogen spring feed around the end of April, and again about five weeks later.

There are basically two kinds of feed: granular ones that may also contain weed killer and moss control, and soluble ones you apply with a watering can or hose dispenser. Granular ones are harder to apply, since you have to be precise or you can get pale 'stripes' where you miss bits out or burn marks where you overdo it. The best thing to do is buy, borrow or hire a little purpose-made trolley with holes in the bottom, and remember to overlap your wheel tracks. I used to use a granular feed for my rather weird-shaped little lawn, and it took some concentration to do it evenly; I had to take the phone off the hook and ignore both children and doorbell while I did it. I eventually worked out that the secret was to wheel the trolley very fast one way, then do it again, this time going across the garden so that it was hard to miss bits. I hated, absolutely hated, doing it, and in the end gave up and started to use soluble feeds. These are not as long lasting, and therefore have to be repeated every few weeks. But in my little garden it was far easier to swing a loaded watering can back and forth as I walked backwards down the lawn. The job was done in a matter of minutes.

So much for the spring feed. The autumn feed, to my mind, is far more important and much less nerve-racking to apply. It is sold specifically as 'Autumn Lawn Feed' and is not interchangeable with the spring one, being low in nitrogen and high in phosphates to strengthen the grass roots for the winter. It does not produce that rush of blood to the head, nor is precision in applying it so important. In fact, if you are really clever, you can mix it in with your top dressing and spread it with a broom. You can also buy soluble autumn lawn food.

If you don't want to feed your lawn at all, then perhaps it is a good idea to leave your lawn clippings on the lawn after mowing just once during the summer. It will eventually break down into some sort of enriching feed, which is apparently better than doing nothing.

Watering

British lawns go brown sometime in July, and go green again in September. If water is in short supply – and we should all treat it as though it is – do not waste it on your lawn. You need an awful lot of water to do the job properly anyway, so look after your new shrubs and trees, but let the lawn do its own thing. The only exception, in my book, is new turf, which is an investment worth protecting. But no-one in their right mind would re-turf a lawn in August, unless it was for a television make-over programme, would they?

Weeds and moss

A healthy, regularly mowed lawn will, in theory, have far less of a weed and moss problem than a neglected and unloved one. And it is certainly true that most weeds peter out if they are mowed all the time. The exceptions are the nasty flat ones such as plantains, dandelions and creeping buttercup. Most of them can be dug out with a kitchen knife, and you can cramp the style of the buttercup by ripping out its runners. Or you could use a spot weeder and apply a lethal dose to the centre of each offender. I really hate using all over weed- or moss-killer, so I don't. I know I am quite irrational about it, but I can't bear the idea of looking at all those bald patches once everything except the grass is dead. I do have patches of weeds here and there, but this is a country garden and the lawn was once a field, so what can I expect? And for part of the year the lushness of the green sward is definitely the result of having a positively disgraceful amount of soft green moss (due to incessant East Sussex winter rain, bad drainage and slightly acid soil). No, I belong quite unashamedly to the 'who cares as long as it's green' brigade.

Finally, whatever your basic attitude to your grass, just about every gardener needs to know how to do some or all of the following:

Reseeding bald patches

Using a hand-fork, loosen the top two inches of soil, perhaps removing some and replacing it with fairly sandy potting compost such as John Innes No. 2. Mix some grass seed with a little of the compost and sprinkle it over the patch, firming it down with your hand or the back of a spade to make it level with the rest of the lawn. Water it *very gently*, using a very fine rose on the watering can. Cover the patch with a piece of chicken wire if you think it might get walked on in the first few weeks after germination (which will be just a matter of days between April to September). When the grass is about 2in high, cut it once with shears. Thereafter you can mow it with the rest. It is important to realize that unless you have addressed the causes of the baldness you will probably have to over-seed (see below) at least once during the growing season.

Transplanting stray grass plants from borders

This is another highly effective (but slightly dotty-sounding) way of coping with small bald patches in the lawn. I call it the Ageing Rock Star treatment (I don't actually, but that's all I can get away with here). I am always weeding lawn-grass plants out of my borders. Instead of ditching them, I trim them and plant them in areas of thin grass or in small bald patches. They actually 'take' very quickly because they already have good roots, and the patch becomes undetectable within a week or so. This is something I used to do a lot and with excellent results in my old small garden.

Over-seeding a tired lawn

In early autumn, once the mowing has slackened off, or in spring before it has gone into top gear, you can over-seed a thin lawn, that is, add fresh seed to the existing lawn without much preparation. I generally add grass seed to top-dressing and do it this way. It does help to thicken things up.

Turf patching

This is a skill I have had to acquire to deal with our rough old country lawn. I mention it here because I am amazed how *un*skilled you need to be to patch your own grass using turf from another part of the same lawn. The point about it is that the grasses automatically 'match', as does the level of soil fertility. It becomes a case of invisible mending within weeks – far better than patching with posh imported turf or re-seeding, which will both take years to blend in. So if you need to re-turf an area, see if you can steal from another part of the lawn. And go on, make that border bigger while you are at it.

CHAPTER 7

Disentangling Roses

Most of us love roses, so there must be something particularly special about them. At one end of the scale, people who generally don't give a fig about plants or flowers start using a soppy voice when they talk about roses – similar to the one they adopt when the subject of the Queen Mum comes up. They may even attempt to grow them on windswept patios in inappropriately small pots that inevitably either dry to a crisp or go completely manky and eventually get chucked away or hidden somewhere with all the other dead things 'round the side'. At the other extreme, gardeners can develop a huge passion for roses, often specializing in growing old shrub roses that only flower for about two or three weeks of the year: the 'pray it doesn't rain, don't blink or you'll miss them' kind of plants, like paeonies. These poor souls relish rolling off the tongue the impossible French names of their favourites – 'Madame de Zees', 'Souvenir de Zatte', and 'Comtessse de Zee Ozère' – to anyone who will listen. It may help your self-esteem to remember that these gardeners can't all be experts, and can probably only remember and pronounce the names of the roses they themselves grow.

In fact, roses are ugly and often troublesome bushes most of which do not fit in with the accepted gardening wisdom that shrubs should have more than one thing going for them in order to earn their keep. Even minimal rose maintenance takes up an extraordinary amount of precious gardening time, time we would far rather spend staring into the pond counting the fish or getting seriously stuck into the renovation of a tired old winter jasmine.

So why does everyone bother? I am sure a lot of it has to do with nostalgia: I grow roses purely for their smell, which to me is definitely a smell of things past. My school emblem was a rose, and once a year all of us pupils would assemble in Bristol Cathedral for the commemoration day service, everyone wearing a rose in their lapel. So the smell of roses is linked in my brain with a feeling of slight nervous excitement. It brings back memories of the smell of the cavernous old stone building, the sound of hymn-singing with a few unfamiliar male voices booming away down there somewhere – and the irritating tickle on the neck caused by several confused greenfly trying to find their way home to our rose garden from the grey landscape of my school blazer. The fact that most roses perform for such a short time makes them even more desirable – how much better strawberries tasted when you could only get them in high summer. And what an old fogey I have become.

The fact is, most people who have a garden have a rose in it somewhere, if only because for sentimental reasons they failed, or have not yet managed, to ditch it. And while it doesn't matter two hoots what the rose is *called*, it does matter that you know what kind of rose it is – be it a hybrid tea, a floribunda, a shrub rose of some kind, or a climber or rambler. Because unless you know at least this much about your roses, you don't know what to expect from them or how to look after them. The first thing I will do, therefore, is give simple basic descriptions of the various rose types. I don't think it is particularly necessary to name names – 'what is what' is more helpful than 'who is who' when it is all a bit of a fog.

The rose boffins have tried to force us to accept a new way of classifying roses, which has not been terribly successful, gardeners being notoriously stubborn about such things. So most of us still divide roses up into broadly the following groups:

Bush roses

These include hybrid tea roses and floribunda (or multicluster) roses bred in the early part of this century after the creation of the National Rose Society and huge upsurge of interest in rose breeding. They are sold by the thousands every year and are the most popular of roses.

Hybrid tea roses
These are tall slim bushes bearing elegant blooms on long stems over a long period during the summer. The flowers are double, often heavily scented and beautifully formed, and are carried singly or with smaller side buds. They are the ideal roses for cutting to put in vases (to go on a beautiful mahogany table, the sunlight from an open casement window filtering though their perfect petals, needless to say). The bushes themselves are difficult to accommodate in a mixed border or a stuffed, shrubby town garden, because of their innate gauntness, and the way in which you have to prune them. Both they and the floribundas (below) look much better grown *en masse* in the sort of rose beds our dads favoured, they can be seen this way, should you wish to do so, in places such as Regents Park, or at the Royal Horticultural Society Rose Garden at Wisley. Generally it is

these bedding roses people inherit from previous owners and need to be 'renovated' or removed because they have become so diseased and ugly through ignorance and/or neglect.

Floribunda or multicluster roses   These are usually, but not always, smaller, wider-spreading bushes that have much more of a rag-bag look to them, with larger clusters of often quite garish flowers that are not generally strongly scented. There are usually two major flushes of flowers in mid- and late summer. Some of these roses are quite useful, adding colour and substance to a mixed border but, again, their natural home is a proper rose bed.

Shrub roses

Shrub roses are quite different in character from bush roses. As the name suggests, these are the roses for a relaxed shrub garden or mixed border, and some are useful for making flowering hedges. There are many different types within this group, for example species roses (wild roses and near relations), modern shrub roses (bred this century with some 'bush rose' parents), old-fashioned roses (bred before this century – a lot of them have those French names), hybrid musk roses and English roses (bred this century with some 'old-fashioned' parents) and rugosa roses from Japan. The whole issue is immensely complicated but the feature these roses generally have in common is their softness of outline. Some flower only once but spectacularly, leaving enormous and decorative hips as a reminder of their splendour. Indeed, roses such as *Rosa glauca* (formerly *Rosa rubrifolia*) are grown chiefly for their orange hips (in this case contrasting well with its thunder-cloud bluish foliage). Many of the shrub roses need a surprising amount of space and only really come into their own if they are allowed it without let or hindrance. Some of them also have very heavy heads when in flower. Tie them, under the arm pits as it were, with twine or raffia to metal or wooden supports to hold them up. Others, such as the popular 'Ballerina', 'Fairy' and 'Magic Carpet' have a very long flowering period and, being small and neat of bloom, can fit into the tiniest of gardens. The best, most useful ones combine a long flowering period, good scent, strong arching growth and a good over-all shape. Many of my own favourites are the hybrid musks ('Penelope', 'Buff Beauty', 'Prosperity', 'Felicia', 'Moonlight' and others – note the generally sensible English names), many of them giving off that heady old-ladies-hand-cream scent. But then, everyone who grows roses (on purpose, that is) has favourites.

Climbing and rambling roses

These are used for climbing and screening purposes. This may sound like stating the obvious, but climbers climb, and ramblers ramble. A lot of gardeners think the names are interchangeable but they aren't. There are important differences when it comes to their type of growth, management and maintenance for reasons which I hope will become clear.

The growth of **climbing roses** forms a woody framework consisting of a few rather stiff stems. The framework changes little once the plant is mature. Many of them have been bred from hybrid tea roses, and, like them, carry single, scented blooms over a very long period. There are two basic types, vigorous – which are often mistakenly referred to as 'ramblers' – and non-vigorous, some of which look like rather stretched hybrid teas and don't climb very far at all. If you wanted to choose a rose to go up a wall or over an arch – to occupy a clearly defined space you should pick one that says 'climber' on the label rather than 'rambler'.

To approach things from the other way, if you have a rose climbing up your house with an enormous rather bare woody base with not much new growth on it, while somewhere under the first floor windows it produces a succession of flowers throughout the summer that you can hardly see, let alone smell, pick or dead-head, this is most probably a maltreated climber.

Unlike climbers, **rambling roses** are generally recognized by their extremely vigorous growth, with several long pliable stems being produced from close to the base of the plant each season. Many of them carry huge and spectactular trusses of, in some cases, rather small flowers over a period of about three weeks in midsummer. Following this they put out a fresh crop of long shoots that, by October, drive any compulsive pruner mad, with often disastrous results for both rose and pruner. Many ramblers are prone to mildew, especially if they are grown on house walls or in other restricted, airless spaces. Another problem with them is that they need tricky midsummer pruning unless grown up trees, which is where they look and perform best. Frankly, if you have a rambler in a place where there is not enough space to allow it to do its own thing, it can be a pain to live with. For midsummer drama, however, ramblers are unsurpassed. It is a bit like living with a loud extrovert.

Pruning Roses

As you might expect, different types of rose require different treatment where pruning is concerned. If you have understood and grasped the basic guidelines for pruning shrubs, it will help considerably in the understanding of rose pruning if you forget all the mystique surrounding the subject and look at roses just as you would other shrubs. Think of them as late or early flowerers that need to be 'renovated' at appropriate times of the year, and encouraged to produce new shoots on which to flower.

Hybrid tea roses, floribundas and climbers fall into the 'late' category, flowering on wood produced in the current year in the same way as, say, a *Buddleia davidii* or a lavender does. They, therefore, should be pruned at some time in the winter or very early spring when they are dormant, so that they can produce new shoots during the late spring that will flower from midsummer onwards.

How to prune bush roses has always been the subject of much discussion among gardeners. My parent's generation – with their traditional rose beds – were happy to hard- prune their hybrid teas and floribundas, cutting them back almost to the ground each year in about February. The results were late- but larger-flowering roses, healthy because they had all the nasty bits automatically cut out of them, but you had to put up with looking at an empty barren landscape for several months of the year.

More recently it has become accepted practice to prune them less hard – to about half their full height, but to be ruthless about cutting out weaker or damaged growth from close to the base of each rose. This is known as 'medium pruning'.

Experiments have been carried out in the past few years pruning roses with hedge trimmers alone. Early results have been amazing, with the bushes flowering profusely. Given the way roses grow, dying back within themselves, congested stems injuring each other with their thorns and becoming prey to disease, I would guess that after a while this method of pruning will fall out of favour, as I can't imagine that, in the long run, this way of pruning will produce anything other than ugly, gradually weakening bushes. Time will tell.

Hybrid tea and floribunda roses ('bush roses') – should be 'medium pruned' between January and March. This is how you do it:

a) Crouch or sit on the ground so you are working on the *base* of the bush. Ignore everything above your head. Don't look up or you might chicken out of what you are about to do.

b) Using sharp secateurs – not the ones you have ruined by cutting garden wire, letting them rust in the rain, etc. – cut out all dead (brown, brittle) and diseased or injured wood from its source and remove from ground level the thickest and brownest stems which are the oldest and therefore the least productive. On a neglected rose, this may be most of what is there, and you may need a small-bladed pruning saw to get though the branches because they are so thick. Don't waver, just do it.

c) Next, cut out all very skinny stems and ones that grow across the bush or touch others.

d) Cut out any immature wood (bendy and with soft thorns) that has grown late in the season from near the base of the bush.

e) Only thick, green and healthy stems should now remain. Cut these down to an outward facing 'eye' or leaf scar – with careful scrutiny you can find one of these on even quite old stems. It is from this scar that the new shoots will come. The cut should be slanting, with the 'eye' about a centimentre below the high point of the slant. The aim is to create a framework of perhaps three or four (in the case of hybrid teas) or half a dozen (in the case of floribundas) vigorous shoots that will form an almost candelabra-shaped bush once they shoot out. The final height of the pruned rose should be about half that of the unpruned bush you started with, which will be somewhere between 30cm and 75cm.

f) Pick up the bits, remove any weeds from around the base of the bush, loosen the top few centimetres of soil carefully with a hand fork, apply rose food and mulch. The truly dedicated will spray the rose with a systemic fungicide such as Nimrod-T which can be absorbed through the stems to prevent mildew, rust and blackspot from developing later in the season.

The key to the whole procedure is to work strictly from the base of the bush. By all means have a tweak about and remove some of the heavy hips and a few inches of top growth before the winter winds buffet everything about, to prevent the roots from loosening. This is not proper pruning, however, and later in the season you have to be much braver than your instincts tell you. The harder you prune a rose, the more it will grow – if a rose is unhealthy, prune it more, not less.

It is very difficult to lay down hard-and-fast rules about pruning roses – particularly climbers and ramblers, because how you do it depends so much on what you want the roses to do for you, how far you want them to climb, how much of their growth you can reach and how bothered you are about their performance. I think it is important, however little you do, that you understand what the plant will do as a result of your action (or inaction).

Climbers should, like bush roses, also be pruned in the winter. The short shoots that have born flowers should be cut back to within a few buds or 'eyes' – leaf scars – of the main woody framework of the plant. To put it another way, this is a relatively simple operation involving cutting back all the shoots that have got hips on them back to short stumps about 10cm long. In the winter if you go and look at a climber that has been pruned by a 'pukka' gardener for years, you will notice an immaculately trained framework of branches, probably attached by neatly tied twine to stout horizontal wires if it is on a wall, with short stumps sticking out off the framework all along its length. This is a far cry from the messes most of us live with, and it is both humbling and educational.

A well-fed, happy climber will generally produce a good stout shoot from near the base every other year or so. Unfortunately, this thick, straight green shoot often looks so at odds with the remainder of the brown, gnarled rose that compulsive pruners frequently shriek 'sucker!' and with a manic gleam in their eyes, cut it (or them) off. What you should actually do is thank your lucky stars the rose has produced such a wonderful thing. As you do so, bend it gently into a position that follows the rest of the framework and tie it in loosely before the end of the summer, by which time it will have become rigid and brittle and may snap if you try to bend it. Come the winter you can then remove one of the old shoots of the framework. This way a climber gradually renews itself and doesn't become an ugly monster, yawning menacingly away from its support and eventually breaking away completely.

If you already have an ugly monster, feed and mulch it for a year and remove the worst and knobbiest shoot from as close to the bottom of the framework as you can. The rose will thus be forced into action once again and you can start to train subsequent new shoots into position and go on from there. Banish axemen pruners from that area of the garden.

In the worst cases – where you have to remove a rose from a house wall or archway in order to carry out building repairs for example – you can, for once, call on the services of that itchy-fingered axeman and cut the whole rose down to the ground to make it start again. You will get no flowers for a year or two while it does, however. This drastic action applies to all kinds of overgrown roses, not just climbers. Old, well-established roses are the most robust of plants and remarkably hard to kill; it is quite difficult to see what all the fuss is about.

So much for the roses that flower on the current season's wood. Next we should look at **ramblers** and **old shrub roses** that flower just once on the previous season's growth. Relating these to the shrub pruning guidelines, they fall roughly into the wiegela or philadelphus category. They therefore need to have their tired flower shoots removed and should be tidied up in mid-season immediately after flowering, to encourage them to produce plenty of new shoots for the following year.

Of these two groups, ramblers are the trickiest, and the vigorous small-flowered varieties the very worst. Since they flower mostly on wood produced at the back end of the previous year, they should be pruned immediately after flowering, unless of course they are growing out of reach up trees or other large structures. It is a devoted soul indeed who gets really stuck in during the hottest part of the year and prunes out the oldest huge shoots of a prickly rambler from ground level and dead-heads the rest, in order to make way for the following year's flowering shoots produced during the surge of new growth that is about to happen. In our London garden, we shared a stunning 'Rambling Rector' (the ultimate extrovert, despite his name) with our lovely neighbours. Pruning him became an annual social event. Everyone used to stand around watching and drinking tea while I teetered up a ladder suffering appalling lacerations. On reflection, real gardeners always have scratched arms.

I have to say that I now bend the rules a bit. I have a half-hearted go during late summer at cutting off any old flowers I can reach as well as thinning out and removing some of the new shoots that appear higher up and make the rose look bothersomely tangled. But I often wait until the rose has lost its leaves in winter, when I can see what I am doing a little better, before cutting out more old wood. I still reserve plenty of long new shoots and tie them in place, which is easy to do since, unlike the shoots of a climber, they remain pliable. There is generally so much new growth produced that I can easily afford to cut out and sacrifice some of it, slim the whole rose down and make a much better fist of the whole job.

What you should definitely not do is 'tidy up' a rambler in the autumn and winter by cutting back all the new shoots that are waving in the breeze. If you do, the following year's flowering will be very much reduced. If you do it every year, the rose will forever have a look of an ugly hedgehog about it.

Many **shrub roses** behave similarly to ramblers in that they are 'early' flowerers, producing blooms on growth made the previous year, and should have old shoots removed after flowering or during the winter when you can get at them better. The newer shoots should be tinkered with as little as possible. But if you become seriously addicted to shrub roses, it is worth finding out more about the pruning of each specific group. Hybrid perpetuals appreciate having their newer stems arched over and pegged down. My beloved hybrid musks need a really good midsummer cut back to encourage a prolific autumn flush of flowers, while some modern shrubs, such as 'Ballerina', should be pruned in the spring more like floribundas, opening out the middle of the bush and cutting it down by about half in early spring. Old shrub roses that flower just once such as species or gallicas are a much simpler kettle of fish. They need very little pruning apart from the winter removal of ancient wood from the base every few years. After their dramatic flush of flowers has finished in midsummer, you should shorten by a little the shoots that have flowered. As with all roses, do not cut off any new growth that comes from the base. If shrub roses have good autumn hips, only remove half of the old flowers – you can go back in the winter and smarten them up by removing any old wrinkled relics that the birds have left behind.

I do appreciate that learning to prune anything from verbal instructions – or even worse, from illustrations in a book – is extremely hard. You go out there armed to the teeth with posh new secateurs, a little shiny saw, your smartest pruning gloves and a brain full of instructions, only to find that somehow your own roses bear absolutely no relation to the ones described and illustrated in your books. Before you know it, your resolve has weakened and you find yourself twiddling around removing a few old rose hips before going off to have a cup of coffee and count the fish again. If at all possible, you should learn by pruning your own roses with someone who knows what they are up to. The Royal Horticultural

Society and some horticulture colleges run pruning demonstrations, which, years ago, I found helpful. But if you really feel confused and care about getting it right, and there is no one to help, take heart. Rome wasn't built in a day. Most of us taught ourselves by trial and error, and roses are very tolerant. Make a note or take pictures of your roses after you have pruned them. If they look ugly or don't flower well one year, do something different the next and you'll get there in the end.

It can be awe-inspiring and very helpful to visit a proper rose garden – Mottisfont Abbey and Sissinghurst Castle for example – and see how many ways there are to train and prune roses. If you go in the winter when the leaves have dropped, you can get a good look at how the training is all done, and maybe even find a friendly gardener whose brains you can gently pick. There is a lot to be learnt about roses.

Buying, Planting and Feeding Roses

There was a time, not so very long ago, when roses were only sold bare-rooted in the winter, and you could not get hold of them at all during the growing season. In fact, this is probably the best way to buy roses. Planted while dormant, they can settle in to their new soil and grow away without a hiccup in the following spring. These days roses are more often presented to us in 2-litre pots at any time of the year, and are often sold in full flower. I think it is worth uttering a word of caution: you should always check, when buying a potted up rose in full leaf or flower, that it has actually been grown in that pot in a good soily compost. Beware of those that were potted up into a peat-based compost at the beginning of the season by the vendor, from stock purchased bare-rooted from a grower.

Roses grown in pots are completely different in character from those that are potted up; they can be planted reasonably safely in the garden during the growing season much as any other container-grown shrub. Since roses do not make a fine network of roots to create a root-ball, you have to take a little extra care as you remove a rose from its pot as you run the risk of much of the soil dropping away and leaving major roots exposed. With a potted-up rose, you have virtually no chance of planting it without all the compost falling away and causing the rose a major headache: it will immediately wilt and possibly die. The best way to check to find out if a rose is a genuine pot-grown rose is to give it a gentle tweak before you buy it. It should feel firm in the pot. If it starts to lift, put the whole pot back where you found it and tiptoe away.

Container-grown roses should be planted in much the same way as other shrubs – with plenty of organic stuff and bonemeal or a special rose fertilizer such as Toprose. If you are planting them bare-rooted make sure there are no broken roots that could rot under ground (cut them off cleanly with secateurs). Make sure you do not end up with an air pocket underneath the plant (fiddle the soil in between the roots carefully with your fingers). Most roses are propagated by being grafted on to wild rootstock, the graft forming a knobbly bit between the roots and stem of the plant. This is a potentially vulnerable part of the rose and after planting should be at soil level, just visible. If it ends up sticking up out of the soil, start your planting process again; likewise if you end up with the graft below soil level. You should avoid being a lazy daisy, trying to build up the soil level around the graft or excavating a small ditch around it and hoping for the best. Take it from me, it does not work.

Subsequent damage below soil level to a grafted rose can result in the production of **suckers**. On standard roses suckers can shoot out of the 'trunk', since the graft knobble is at the top, where the rose branches out. Suckers are identifiable by looking at the overall colour of the shoot, and not necessarily, as is popularly believed, by counting the number of leaflets. Suckers are generally a pale, matt colour, quite different from the darker, shinier leaves of their hosts. They should always removed, because being part of a vigorous wild rose they can sap away the strength of the grafted rose and overwhelm it. The chances are that, if you have a wild rose growing in your garden, it is a sucker that has taken over from a maltreated and neglected cultivated rose. If you prune off a sucker, even below soil level, it will shoot from lower dormant buds and you will probably get two more as a reward for your efforts. The answer is to trace them back to the root from which they have sprung and wrench them off, destroying as you do so the possibility of the sucker growing from another bud.

Most roses need sun, hate draughty corners, like growing in heavy-ish soil that is never waterlogged, and seem to be happiest in soil with a neutral pH, although they will cope with acid or limey soil. Roses, once established, develop into extremely tough, strong-rooted plants that can live and flourish for thirty years or more. They are quite vulnerable for the first year or so and should be checked every spring to make sure that they have not loosened in the soil; they should be trodden well in if they have.

The usual advice that you should prune down a newly planted rose is one that is very hard to follow, but generally worth taking. If a rose has been grown in a container, the growth can often be twisted and spindly. By pruning it right down in the first spring, you can kick start its growth anew. This is particularly important with climbing roses, which need a good stout framework from the start. I have been far too impatient in the past to see a rose do something pretty in its first season, and have often regretted not being more strong minded. Mind you, there was that memorable occasion when I did do everything right, and had to wait for the best part of eighteen months to see a rose flower for the first time, only to find that it had been mislabelled. Much cursing ensued, but as is so often the way with plants and gardens, if not in other parts of one's life, the gate crasher proved to be the life and soul of the party. I never actually bothered to find out who the interloper was – it was a scented shrub rose that flowered twice each year – but it was absolutely wonderful.

Roses appreciate a feed twice a year, in March and July, with a proper rose fertilizer. In my experience, to try to simplify things by giving them a balanced feed along with the rest of the garden results in less than perfect growth. Rose food is higher in potash which makes roses flower really well; it also contains various trace elements that they appreciate. Roses also appreciate a mulch with organic stuff in spring and, if possible, again in midsummer; they particularly enjoy having their feet covered with well-rotted horse manure. I have also used a soluble rose feed which seemed excellent, but had to be applied once a week during the entire growing season, thereby providing the overstretched gardener with something else to remember to do. I instinctively feel, however, that the soluble feed hits the spot better during the dry weather of high summer, after the roses have had their first flush of flower. The recommended July granular feed needs to be rained on or otherwise watered, in or it can just sit on the surface and do nothing.

Pests and Problems

Elsewhere, when dealing with pests and diseases I have outlined most of the troubles that can afflict roses and mentioned solutions and remedies. The most serious pests are aphids and leafhoppers, and the most difficult diseases to control are mildew, blackspot and rust. I regret to say that I have personally never seen perfect roses grown without the use of chemical sprays. The all-in-one cocktail rose sprays such as Roseclear simplify the whole pest/disease control issue, but if any one problem takes serious hold or develops a resistance you can chop and change with your chemicals, which means reading all the small print. Roses occasionally suffer from iron-deficiency chlorosis which can be sorted out with a dose of Sequestrene, and sometimes suffer from physiological disorders – mineral defficiency, for example – that can be sorted out by starting to use a proper rose fertilizer.

I hate to be harsh about plants that have such a special place in our affections, but in my view it all comes down to the inescapable fact that if you love roses, alas, you have to work at them. And if you haven't got time to work at them, you shouldn't grow them.

CHAPTER 8

The Undesirables — Pests, Diseases and Weeds

i will come clean straight away. As far as pests and diseases are concerned I reserve all my best 'green' practices strictly for my vegetable garden. I feel it simply does not make sense to go to the trouble of growing gorgeous vegetables that you can prepare and eat minutes after picking on a patch of land that has been subjected to chemical warfare. So as well as treating the soil organically, I use no chemical pest controls. I look the other way if a few contented caterpillars give me the slip and munch their way lazily around my purple-sprouting broccoli, and put up with having to wash whole armies of aphids off the ruby chard. There is plenty for all of us, I say through gritted teeth, as I water some foul-smelling, home-made organic nettle brew into the soil, wondering all the while how this vile stuff helps to produce what are to us the sweetest, most wonderful tasting tomatoes we have ever eaten.

In the rest of the garden it is a different story. For, alas, I find it necessary to kill some pests and treat some diseases with chemicals. Flower gardens are a contrived manipulation of things natural, and however nurturing you are by nature, however 'green' you try to be, sometimes it is not enough to turn a blind eye, and not practical to pick off pests by hand. You have to be tough on the undesirables or your shrubs may shrivel and your borders may be bitten to bits. This attitude, I feel sure, is bound to infuriate the 'all or nothing' organic brigade. Who knows, I may yet change – like many gardeners I am far more sparing with the spray bottle than I used to be a few years ago. But this is where I am with the whole issue at the moment, and this is the standpoint from which I write this chapter.

Pests and Diseases

All in all, it would be daft of me to try to give you in one small chapter the complete story on the eradication of every garden pest you are likely to meet. So what I aim to do is highlight the most troublesome and often encountered pests and problems to help you to identify more clearly what is what, and minimize the number of nasty things in bottles and packets collecting dust on a spidery shelf in the back of your garden sheds, by paring them down to a fairly simple 'kit' of products that I have used successfully myself.

In my experience, the vast and constantly changing array of chemicals on sale serves to confuse. Just to give one example, while checking my facts for this chapter, I discovered that two pest killers from two different manufacturers, Sybol Extra from Scotts and Polysect from Solaris, contain exactly the same chemical. The original Sybol – which has been around for as long as I have been aware – contained something completely different.

Experts in the field of 'pestandiseasology' will tell you that as each vile beast develops immunity to a chemical, it is necessary to find another that will do a similar job, hence the stuffed shelves in the garden centres. Furthermore, every year it seems that some or other chemical is banned so we have to learn all about something new. It can all seem, therefore, a bit of an expensive nightmare the understanding of which requires a lot of reading of that very small print on packaging again, which most of us are far to lazy to do.

To give them their due, the big chemical companies have got wind of the fact that the general gardening public doesn't much enjoy all this chemical stuff, and are starting to sell us ready-mixed, rather pricey, user-friendly bottles of this and that with easy to understand instructions (and extravagant claims) clearly marked on them. This is helpful if you have a tiny garden and very few pests, but most of us (if we use sprays at all) would find this an expensive solution, as it were, to the pest/disease problem.

With great difficulty – since I am as scientifically dyslexic as they come – I have put together a basic pest-and-blight kit with no difficult names, of products that you are *currently* likely to need on a fairly regular basis. Rapid, Polysect or Tumblebug are insecticides that between them should cover all the common leaf pests. Tumbleblight II, Nimrod-T or Spotless are systemic fungicides. Roseclear 2 is a systemic insecticide combined with systemic fungicide – a cocktail of the chemicals in Rapid and Nimrod-T. Liquid Slugit and/or slug pellets do exactly what you might imagine, and finally, for plants in containers, Plant Pins.

If you have not already got one, you should also get a 1.25-litre pump spray bottle, as made by Hozelock.. You should, however, always remember the following:

Don't mix up too much solution (hence the advice that you should only get a small spray bottle). Once mixed up, fungicides – that kill fungal diseases and blights – and pesticides (you understand that one) cannot be stored, unlike the ready-to-use ones mentioned above. If you mix up too much solution, you will be tempted to use the excess where it is not strictly necessary or tip it down the domestic drain system, which is a no-no. (You should, in fact, spray any excess mixture on to waste ground and wash it away with additional water).

Don't spray in strong sunshine, high winds, or near ponds, pets and, of course, children.

Don't forget to wear some protection for your skin, and wash thoroughly after you have finished, including your face. No-one realistically expects gardeners to don a full space-suit to spray a couple of roses, but wearing gloves, a mask, and long-sleeved and long-legged clothing is a sensible precaution.

Don't go looking for trouble. Small, airless and muggy inner city gardens do get very pest- and disease-ridden it is true. The lack of winter frost and sharp cold winds means that certain bugs are active virtually all the year round and their numbers are not naturally reduced by fluctuating seasonal temperatures. However, there is a natural balance in the garden, a sort of 'bug-eat-bug' situation. You can upset this balance easily so that a pest becomes a plague if you knock out all its natural predators. So try to turn a blind eye to pests unless they actually disfigure the garden. Seek out and use selective pesticides, and don't career round the garden too often, Rambo-style, with the spray bottle.

Do use the recommended doses – follow instructions on the packaging *to the letter*. Making up a solution 'extra strong' can harm your plants.

Do use systemic chemicals where possible. These are ones that are actually absorbed by plants, making them unpalatable or immune to the pest or disease in question. The effects last far longer than with purely contact sprays (though generally not as long as the manufacturers claim) in addition to killing off breeding adults, you clobber most of the next generation of each pest as well. With contact sprays, you have to almost literally hit each bug in the eye, and drenching every leaf on each side is an unrealistic aim.

Do run a tight ship. Clear away blighted leaves, cut down plants with pests such as spider mite that you have failed to control.

Bag up or burn all the nasty bits, and every so often clear up old stacks of plant pots and the bits behind the shed that you would rather not look at. Heaven forbid that I should encourage anyone to be one of those gardeners who spend whole weekends hoovering the borders and power-jetting the patio, but a little sensible tidiness goes a long way towards creating a less pesty environment.

The following list starts with the most common pests and diseases, and ends with the hardest to treat. It is not intended to be comprehensive. There are loads of illustrated books by real experts on the subject and if you cannot identify a problem someone at your local garden centre or nursery may be able to help (take freshly collected specimens in clear, sealed plastic bags). It is worth joining the Royal Horticultural Society just to use their free diagnosis and advice service.

Aphids is the name that covers all those green, black or rusty-red, winged or wingless sap-sucking insects found in frantically gyrating clusters at the tips of new shoots. After mild winter, aphids can get going surprisingly early so be on guard from February onwards. They can be severely damaging especially to early-flowering honeysuckles, where attacks by blackfly can go unseen actually within the shoot tips. They are nearly always found on roses, chiefly in the first half of the summer. They also attack the new shoots of shrubs that are produced after mid-season pruning – for example, the new growth of philadelphus can be virtually destroyed by infestations of blackfly in July. Spray with Rapid, which acts by contact as well as being systemic, and doesn't harm ladybirds, bees or lacewings (all garden good-boys). Roseclear 2 contains an aphid killer as well as a fungicide (see paragraphs below on mildew and blackspot).

   Almost as if by magic, since moving to the country I have not been plagued to any great extent by aphids on my roses in spring. Either the enormous bird population, which includes hoards of hungry blue-tits, is doing its job or my eyesight is getting worse. I once had a student who, shunning the use of chemicals in her garden, used to swear blind she had no aphids in her London garden. I discovered the secret of her success: she used to remove her specs when she went out into the garden. Voilà – no pests.

Slugs and snails are chiefly active during damp weather. In dry weather you can find them in huge gangs in old ivy, around the compost heap and almost interleaved in stacks of empty clay pots, so this is a good time to round them up. In winter, water the borders with Liquid Slugit to get the small black soil-dwelling slugs that eat roots and bulbs. I have experimented by mixing Liquid Slugit in a spray bottle (you have to keep shaking it or it clogs up) and spraying upwards into an ivy-covered wall in order to try to get contol of a really bad infestation in a town garden. At other times I find it best to use pellets. Those containing methiocarb (such as Slug Gard) are more lethal than those with metaldehyde (Slugit). I have known major snails to recover from the effects of metaldehyde pellets and shimmy off into the border – presumably with a bad hangover – for another hosta binge. Should your slugs and snails become tolerant of one type, switch to another. But if you don't like using slug pellets – any many of us do not – round them up and drop them in salty water, which will kill them quite quickly. If all this murder and mayhem is an anathema to you, go out on a damp night with a torch and catch them in the act, put them in a bag and drive them to your local open space or park. I have heard a rumour that they come back the next day.

Whitefly are actually tiny white moths living on the underside of leaves. They are mainly a greenhouse or conservatory pest, but do enjoy enclosed and sheltered areas in mild gardens, where they proliferate particularly on climbers and wall shrubs. As soon as you see trouble, you should spray with Tumblebug or Polysect, whichever proves more lethal · to your particular strain of whitefly. You will probably have to repeat the process at fairly frequent intervals. I sometimes use Plant Pins (expensive impregnated pieces of card that look a little like book matches) that you shove into the soil around indoor or container plants, preferably before a bad infestation takes hold. You should be warned that there are some new super whitefly around that are seemingly resistant to the normal pesticide treatments. Somebody, somewhere, will come up with a solution soon, I have no doubt.

Leafhoppers also live on the underside of leaves, and are often confused with whitefly. If you look closely, however, they look more like tiny greenish grasshoppers with big wings. When disturbed, they have a less dizzy mothy flight pattern than whitefly. In town gardens they seem to do most damage on roses and tobacco plants. Leafhoppers disfigure leaves by sucking sap and making them appear slightly bleached. There is a super-huge leafhopper that hangs out around rhododendrons in midsummer and can spread the fungal spores that cause bud blast (black, slightly bristly flower buds that fail to open) on rhododendrons. It is definitely worth having a go at this one, and at the same time you should try to remove any old blackened buds that are still attached to the bushes. Leafhoppers are immune to the chemical in Rapid, so you have to spray with Tumblebug or Polysect, as for whitefly.

Froghoppers make 'cookoo-spit' when they are tiny in spring, most noticeably on lavender and rosemary. The 'spit' eventually disappears, by which time the ugly little nymphs have become just as ugly brown, hopping, frog-like bugs that suck sap and do a lot of damage.

If you can bear it, pick them off by hand and squash them when they are still in the 'spit', which unfortunately acts as an effective shield against any chemicals and natural predators.

Caterpillars eventually become beautiful butterflies and moths, and unless your garden is being seriously eaten up, be merciful. If the problem is intolerable, it really is easiest to pick them off by hand, since they generally attack one plant at a time. You could try squashing the eggs that butterflies lay on the backs of leaves. If you have a massive caterpillar attack, on a honeysuckle or on nasturtiums for example, you can stun them with Polysect so that they drop to the ground. You still have to collect them up and destroy them or they might just wake up, shrug their shoulders and walk off into the sunset.

Woodlice do little harm in tidy gardens, since they mostly eat decaying organic matter, and are of course vital members of the compost heap team. Occasionally they start to breed and make a nuisance of themselves around low, woody plants such as helianthemums, and in wooden barrels. If you hate them, clean up your garden. If you find them trekking across your hall, investigate for dry rot which they also eat.

Scale insects are hard to eradicate. There are many different types, but the most common are brown and limpit-like and are found on the stems or the backs of leaves of certain garden shrubs – bay, cornus, camellia and photinia, for example. They can also take hold on indoor plants. Treatment is difficult because of their 'armour plating'. If I detect them early enough on indoor plants I use Plant Pins (you usually only become aware of them because they drip a sticky substance on to leaves below them). Or I stroke them off the leaves and branches with cotton wool dipped in methylated spirits or a solution of various insecticides in turn, to see which one works. On major outdoor shrubs, where their secretions often form an ugly black sooty coat on evergreen leaves, I think the secret is to shift as many of them as possible out of position with a gloved finger or hand, and then spray the entire bush with Tumblebug while they are vulnerable. You can then try washing evergreens with a dilute solution of washing-up liquid, if the look of the leaves really offends you and you have time for such housewifely gardening.

Capsid bugs are long-leggedy beasties that move so fast that they are hardly ever seen, but can be devastating to certain late-flowering shrubs, notably fuchsia and caryopteris. They nibble at flower buds from within, resulting sometimes in a total lack of blooms, with shoot tips puckered and holed, and collapsed. On susceptible plants, try to remember to spray with Tumblebug at regular intervals during the summer. In my experience, however, by the time you notice the damage, it is usually too late and the capsid bugs will be over the hills and far away.

Leafminers are grubs that burrow into leaves, leaving grey tracks showing on their surfaces. They are particularly harmful to the chrysanthemum family, which includes feverfew and those ubiquitous potted marguerites. Spraying with Polysect has an almost immediate effect.

Lily beetles are bright scarlet; they nibble the petals and leaves of lilies, completely ruining them. They occur mainly in the south of England, but are marching steadily northwards. Whenever you see them, usually in fornicating pairs, you should spoil their fun by picking them off the lilies and stamping on them. Look out for their vile, slimy grubs on the leaves as well, which someone once (accurately) described to me as looking like pulsating bird-poo. Dust soil round lilies with something which claims to be 'Weevil Killer' (Gamma BHC dust – rather nasty) in spring, if you want to feel you are doing something positive. I fear, however, that the 'seek and stamp' (SAS) method of control is the only one that really works. It helps, I find, to grow lilies in big pots near a well-used thoroughfare, where you will spot the first sign of trouble as you pass by.

As you may have guessed from the above venomous description, I have had considerable trouble with lily beetle in my time.

Earwigs have a knack of hiding in the middle of many-petalled flowers and having a wonderfully destructive munching session. If disturbed, they drop to the ground and run off at high speed. You have to trap them, which is not hard since they are such compulsive hiders. Corrugated cardboard, rolled round a stick, or a small bundle of straw stuck in an upturned flower pot on top of a cane, can both prove to be irresistible to a shortly-to-be-squashed earwig. Basically it is just a more elaborate version of SAS, as with the lily beetle above.

Worms on lawns can be a problem, especially in the autumn on damp shady areas. They produce numerous worm casts (which my son aptly called 'worm castles') on which you inevitably tread, creating patches of fine mud that look ugly and seem to act as magnets for dandelion seeds. Chlordane and Carbaryl – the chemicals available until recently for worm control – are now both banned. Buy a besom (witch's broom) and sweep the casts off the lawn regularly. And try hard to think warm thoughts about worms, who are our very best garden friends.

Mildew appears most commonly in the form of a downy coating on the stems and leaves of many garden plants – roses, asters, phlox and apple trees, to maim (sorry, name) but a few. However, there are many kinds of mildew, and they tend to be specific to each plant. If you have mildew on your apples, for example, it will not spread to your phlox or to your roses. Some – those that attack honesty and *Allysum saxatile* for example, merely cause puckering on the upper sides of leaves, so that it is not until you inspect the undersides that you actually see the thick patches or blisters of white down.

Mildew is often caused by over-crowding resulting in the lack of circulation of air around leaves and stems, and dry roots. Some plants are very susceptible, and if they suffer one year, unless you cure the problem, you will certainly have it the next year. Mildew usually does not become evident until about July, and prevention by spraying before that time is definitely easier than trying to cure the problem once it has taken hold and has started to disfigure plants. Spray with the systemic fungicide Nimrod-T, and if plants fail to respond to treatment try Tumbleblight II or Spotless.

Blackspot is a fungus that attacks roses, especially those suffering from general neglect. The first sign is a small black spot on some of the lower leaves of the rose. The spot enlarges and the rest of the leaf turns yellow. Affected leaves then drop off. Severely diseased roses can be killed. Spray roses – particularly those you know to be infected from the previous year – with Tumbleblight II or Nimrod-T or Spotless, starting the moment the shoots start to appear. Roseclear 2 also contains a fungicide for mildew. When you are pruning, remove any shoots you see with black or purple streaks or spots on them. Make sure you pick up as many of the dropped leaves as possible, the spores can be held in the soil from one year to the next, and you can find you are dogged by the problem of blackspot permanently.

Rust takes the form of orange spores on the backs of leaves. It is most troublesome – virtually incurable – on hollyhocks. You can spray with one of the systemic fungicides mentioned above for mildew and blackspot from early spring, as the leaves emerge. Or you could religiously remove affected leaves in an attempt to control its spread, or you could just treat hollyhocks as a very short lived perennial and replace them every other year, since the older the plant the worse the problem seems to get.

Rust also attacks roses, but is more easily controlled. In fact mildew, blackspot and rust on roses can be dealt with by using Roseclear 2, which also contains an insecticide. If you do not have any leaf pests, however, you could just use one of the fungicides listed above.

And now for the very worst …

Spider mites are truly horrid microscopic mites. They are often called red spider, but are neither red, nor spider-like. The first sign of infestation is a bronzing and curling of leaves of various herbaceous plants and shrubs. If you get a really bad infestation, you can actually see the mites shinning up and down the tiny webs they spin between the leaflets on affected plants. Entire plants can curl up and die back and, in the case of shrubs and especially roses, drop all their leaves completely. All this happens when you least want it to, in July.

Spider mites used to be almost exclusively a greenhouse problem, and were managed with fumigants and winter wash-downs. They are virtually impossible to control in the garden. In towns, they are practically epidemic because of drought (which encourages their breeding), milder winters (increasing numbers of female mites overwinter to breed the following summer), coupled with the fashion for overcrowded borders. Always inspect plants you buy or are given for telltale signs – a sandy-orange dust (not spotty, like rust) on the undersides of leaves. Throw away any herbaceous plants that are obviously affected or at the very least cut them back hard and burn the trimmings and give them a good feed with a soluble fertilizer such as Miracle-Gro, to put renewed lead in their pencils. Moisten the leaves of your plants in the evening during hot spells, to discourage the mites from breeding so fast.

I have had minimal success with chemical control of spider mites. You could try frequent spraying with Polysect. Or you could move house.

Vine weevils are hooked-legged, black nocturnal beetles with long snouts, which eat characteristic 'U'-shaped holes in the edges of leaves and petals at night. They often infest azalea and rhododendron beds, adore euonymous and bergenia, and can reduce whole areas of the garden to rags but you hardly ever see them. Indeed, if you do see one slowly walking across your living room wall, check the soil in your houseplants since these nasty creatures lay eggs in the soil around certain favoured plants, frequently those in containers. The eggs hatch into vile, white, crescent-shaped maggots, just under 1cm long, which then eat away entire roots of plants. The first you know about their presence is that pansies, busy Lizzies, and the wonderful *Heuchera* 'Palace Purple', for example, collapse completely. When you touch them to look for the source of the problem, you find that they have no roots at all: whole plants just come away in your hand like so many unstuck toupées. If your containers become infested with grubs – you can't miss them once you start investigating – you should pick them out and throw away the compost. I put any grubs I find in the middle of the lawn for the robins to take away and feed to their young.

Until recently, any attempt at chemical control seemed useless. I used to resort to going out at dead of night, holding a tea-tray under the particular rhododendron that was a known haunt of my evil weevil gang. I would bash the bush, and down would tumble the nasty nocturnal revellers. I would then run like hell with my loaded tea-tray and tip them all down the waste disposal unit in the kitchen. I would turn the 'on' switch with great gusto, having in one fell swoop interrupted the life-cycle of one of my most dreaded horticultural enemies. Who ever said that gardeners were nice, gentle people?

Incidentally, I used to pass on this remarkably successful method of control of vine weevil to my students. On one occasion, one wide-eyed class-member, American as I recall, inquired earnestly if a drinks tray would work as well.

I am happy to say that there are now some much more sensible and effective alternatives to the above batty atrocity. Recently developed and now available to gardeners is Plant Protection Compost, a growing medium which contains, the manufacturers claim, an effective chemical control for vine weevil, if renewed annually. This potentially knocks the weevil problem on the head in greenhouses, and for plants in containers. There are also biological controls in the form of dormant nematodes (microscopic predators of weevil grubs) which can be mixed with water and added to soil and composts where they will start to go to work (almost literally) on destroying the grubs at 'grass root level', as it were. The nematodes should be applied to containers and plants in the ground outside in late August, when the soil is warm. One way or the other, the dreaded weevil may have had his chips.

Rats cannot be classified as one of the very worst garden problems, you are quite right, even though it is said that in our towns we are never more than three metres from one. However, by including them in this list, I have the opportunity to illustrate another problem, that is namely general dippiness, also known as a lack of common sense.

My dear former neighbour in London appeared early one morning on my doorstep quite distraught – there is no need to say what she was wearing, of course. We often communicated on matters horticultural early in the day, mutually unclad. She begged me to inspect a series of large round holes that had appeared, apparently during the previous twenty-four hours, in her front garden, as she was convinced that they were caused by rats. In her defence, I have to say that as I recall she was pregnant, and that therefore the space between her ears that normally accommodated a larger than average brain had perhaps been temporarily occupied by one of those excesses of fluids that seem to slosh around the body at such times. Anyway, she calmly returned to her house once I had pointed out that the window cleaner had been around the day before, and perhaps… maybe… could his ladder… just possibly…?

Viruses are incurable. There are numerous viruses that affect plants. They generally cause puckering, stunting and mottling of leaves, and the only thing to do if you suspect a plant has a virus is dig it up and burn it. Sap-sucking insects spread viruses, so an obvious precaution is to take great care to prevent aphid attacks on particularly vulnerable plants, notably clematis and lilies.

A final word about **biological control of pests** as mentioned above. Biological (as opposed to chemical) control is basically the way forward if you object, and we all increasingly do, to using so many chemicals to control nasties in our garden. It is a term that is applied to the exploitation of the 'dog-eat-dog' aspect of the pest world, and involves introducing natural predators of a given pest into a controllable environment and letting them do their worst. Apart from the vine-weevil control, most of the controls available involve flying or crawling parasites, and are only practical for use in greenhouses and conservatories. The Royal Horticultural Society produces leaflets with the latest information on biological pest control. It is an area in which there is much research being done, and it is definitely a space to be keenly watched.

Weeds

I had a husband once – the father of my erstwhile sticky-fingered plane-spotter son – who in the absence of a lawn to mow or a hedge to trim, became obsessed with the only major weed in our tiny garden, that unstoppable little urban invader, oxalis. So great was his distaste for this minuscule three-leaved irritation, that he would move heaven and earth, destroying four square yards of stoutly emerging herbaceous treasures in my little border in the process, if he saw as much as a single specimen popping up. Like many unequal gardening partnerships, we used to bicker endlessly about such things. When we split up (not for purely horticultural reasons), he moved to Paris and lived in a flat, so France was thus spared his uncontrollable marauding garden habits. He has now moved to Belgium and is acquiring a house with, I hear, a substantial patch of potentially attractive greenery. Heaven only knows what will happen if Brussels sprouts.

The point of the story, apart from having a gentle dig (no pun intended this time), is that some of us really care, and others really don't, about weeds. And the smaller the garden, the more we are likely to care, because even the most unobtrusive of weeds has a tendency to glare at us, as do slug holes in the hostas, every time we go out into a tiny garden where, as we all know, 'every leaf matters'.

A lot depends on how you define the term 'weed'. People with big gardens are quite blasé about them, only snapping into action with a hand-fork or a bottle of weedkiller if nasty perennials like ground elder dare to produce flowers in the middle of a posh border, or bind-weed surprises them with a jovial wave from the top of an apple tree. (There is too much to do, they will tell you archly, without getting picky about things like weeds). But for most of us, you could say that a weed is *any* plant that invades the territory of other, more delicate ones, spoiling the way they look and threatening their existence. Even something as gentle and pleasant as that lovely, papery, pale-yellow Welsh poppy can be seen as a weed if it overwhelms your alpines, while if it gently infiltrates the cracks between some shady paving stones beneath sombre trees it could be viewed as a bit of a bonus, a plant to be encouraged, even.

So what can you do if you are have a real weed problem, or you are just a bit of a weedophobe?

One of the first rules you should make for yourself is *never let a real weed flower*, for obvious reasons. So, at the first sight of a bold yellow dandelion, rip off its head. You can deal with the rest of the plant later. If the dandelion has already formed a 'clock', crunch the head in the palm of your hand as you grasp it and dispose of it carefully, or it will release its seeds to the wind. (Garden neurotics may well find themselves, an hour or so later, trying to fasten a rose tie or open a fertilizer packet still clutching a clammy paw full of such treasures, having totally forgotten what it is in their hand and why it is there, but still holding on for grim death anyway). The NLRWF rule is a bit of a hard one to stick to if, for example, you regard prolific seeders like forget-me-nots or the afore-mentioned Welsh poppy as weeds. In this event, you may want to enjoy the flowers, but then have to stop them dropping their seeds everywhere, which means you have to be quick off the mark after they have flowered, either pulling the whole plant out of the ground (forget-me-nots), or dead-heading them with a passion (poppies).

Incidentally, if your forget-me-nots are only a problem because they are in the *wrong* place, pull them up very gently just as they are going to seed, and shake them upside down in the *right* place, and hey presto. You can do this with all sorts of self-seeders.

The second rule is to familiarize yourself with your weedlings. Learn to recognize bogeymen when they are mere bogeybabies, when eradication is far easier. I am thinking here of real monster-raving-loony weeds such as dock, thistles, that borage-like blue flowered hairy thing called alkanet (so many of us nurture these thinking they are foxgloves, but *feel* the difference, only if it is silky is it a foxglove) and any dandelions that manage to slip through your net. If you recognize them early, you can whip them out with no trouble. If you miss them and they get their roots down deep, your weed obliteration programme moves into a whole different league.

The third rule is to remember weed seeds can lie dormant in the soil for years, germinating only when they are offered the right combination of light, moisture, warmth and so on. If your garden has suffered from years of neglect, the chances are your topsoil is full of dormant seeds just waiting to snap into action and torment you. It makes sense in these circumstances, if you are planning a major planting project, to wait a few weeks after your initial purge and soil preparation. Let the first generation of weed seeds you have brought to the surface germinate, and either weedkill them with glyphosate or hoe them off at the ankles, disturbing the soil as little as possible. The longer you leave the area alone before you plant, the more weeds you will be able to destroy this way. You may even feel sufficiently motivated to apply a weed-smothering mulch after you have done your planting.

What about weedkillers?

I have to confess to being a totally irrational wimp where weedkillers are concerned, so feel somewhat unqualified to urge others to use them. Time and time again I have tried to get over the problem. I know, or I think I know, that used to the limited extent in the way that gardeners generally do, the latest generation of weedkillers sold to us are environmentally far less damaging than insecticides, yet I would still rather hand-weed than use a chemical. Parts of our new garden have serious infestations of nettle, ground elder, dock, thistle, escaped rampant mint and just about every other thug in the book. And quite apart from my rather irrational distaste for sprays on environmental grounds, I know from experience that in among the weeds in the derelict borders are seedlings or remnants of nice things I really want to keep.

There are, of course, horses for courses. There are weedkillers that will kill newly cut tree-stumps with one application (Root Out) and then break down in the soil and are, it is claimed, harmless to the environment. One of the 'safest' weedkillers is the powerful glyphosate (found in Roundup and Tumbleweed) that reaches tough perennial roots through the leaves, but similarly does not linger in the soil. For patches of really well-established perennial weeds such as nettles or docks in rough grass (not lawns or borders) there are the selective weedkillers SBK or Verdone. Products that contain the really rather nasty diquat and paraquat (Weedol) will attack annual weeds almost instantly, but you can sow seeds on the site you have treated soon afterwards, whereas weedkillers that also contain simazine (Pathclear) will inhibit the future germination of seedlings, so have an effect that lasts for several weeks.

I have a horror of getting weedkillers on to neighbouring plants, and I find that it is hard to use any of them in spray form without running the risk of them 'drifting' invisibly. Nevertheless I have used Roundup (glyphosate) via a watering can to eradicate a huge re-growth of annual and perennial weeds in an area I had gutted and needed to plant up in a hurry. Similarly I have used Pathclear on a weedy gravel drive and an old brick path that was so grassy that it had almost been absorbed into the neighbouring lawn. I also occasionally buy a big bottle of 'ready-mixed' glyphosate. Through a home-made cowl created from a chopped-up mineral-water bottle I spray individual weeds on the drive or paths and thus minimize the risk of the chemicals drifting on to anything important. I have to say that on each occasion the weedkillers worked brilliantly, saving me an enormous amount of time and immeasurable effort.

Despite this, in order to avoid using weedkillers regularly, I blitz the ground elder and nettle whenever I can, forking out great mats of white or yellow running roots respectively and burning them, or letting them completely dry out in the sun before putting them in a very rough compost pile at the far end of the garden reserved exclusively for undesirables. This makeshift heap might, just might, be itself weedkilled one day and the coarse compost used as a mulch for the orchard trees, but I doubt if I will ever trust it in the garden proper.

After these purges I find that as long as I return to the patch and have another go at it within a month or two, the left-behind scraps that have regrown are relatively easy to weed out, particularly when the soil is dry. The weed problem is definitely far less bad than it was a year ago, but if I were to miss a season for some reason, it would start to get worse again.

The accepted wisdom is that you should mulch thickly where you have ground elder, which tends to have roots that stay near the soil surface. The roots will snuggle upwards into the soft layer of mulch and can then be removed wholesale. Others say you should weaken it by watering it with sequestered iron, or paint or spot weed it with glyphosate. Or, where the weeds are not entangled with other, wanted plants, you can cover the area with black plastic for up to a year in order to starve them into submission. This works really well (except that in my garden all the local moles treated the area as a sort of moley Centre Parcs and had a whale of a time in there, driving my ever-vigilant cat mad). If you can't stand looking at black plastic, you can always hide it with a layer of bark chippings for as long as it takes.

Whilst I find myself waging a constant war with nettles, I have had to teach myself to be fairly laid back where ground elder is concerned, since much of it is concentrated in borders that I am not inclined to gut and replant at the moment because of lack of time. This in fact does not present such a crisis, for while ground elder is quick off the mark to show early on in the season – and could in fact be sprayed with glyphosate if one was similarly quick of the mark – other more lofty perennials soon come up through it and disguise its presence. So maybe that is actually the answer. Grow plenty of bold plants – in my experience *Crocosmia* 'Lucifer' does well in this department, as do day lilies, some of the big asters and *Chrysanthemem maximum*. Every few years, you may have to dig up clumps and pull out the very visible and obvious white roots of the elder. But since you tend to split up major clumps of things every few years anyway, you have the chance to have a purge on these occasions – and then just carry on turning a blind eye. This is perhaps not really what you want to read in a gardening book, or maybe it is.

Bindweed is another headache weed, every scrap of root left in the soil capable of becoming an independent, upwardly-spiralling nightmare within a season. As with my attempts at control of ground elder and nettle, I also deal with bindweed by digging it out where possible, but since its roots seem to have gone to earth under the large sandstone rocks that punctuate our clay-soiled garden, this is an uphill struggle. It is impossible to ignore bindweed with its big white flowers in late summer, so I also rip at it a lot and never let it get very far up into my plants. The problem doesn't seem to be getting any worse, so the combination of digging and ripping seems to be adequate for the time being. The sensible advice I give but don't follow (because it looks hideous) is to put canes in the border, encourage the bindweed to climb up them, then weedkill it with a glyphosate/wallpaper glue mix (so it doesn't drip). Alternatively, you can detach the bindweed from its host plants very carefully, stuff bundles of it, still attached to its roots, into plastic bags and spray glyphosate in to them. You can then hide the bags full of the dying menace under other plants in your border.

To sum up: I know that I can, with the passage of time, by being vigilant, and by hand-weeding, get to grips with the annual weeds in my garden if I care enough to do so. I also know that all things being equal, I am unlikely to be able to eradicate completely my tough perennial weeds without the use of a weedkiller such as glyphosate. Provided I have the energy, I will probably be able to control them to a reasonable degree by digging and ripping periodically.

Oddly enough, one of the things that stops me using weedkillers on my really tough perennial weeds is the certain knowledge (even the manufacturers of the products warn you about this) that one treatment will maim, but will not kill outright. The thought of looking at all those wizened, deformed leaves and then watching the weeds re-grow, and having to go through that spraying again is too much for me, but, as I say, I am irrational about it.

CHAPTER 9

Propagation Without a Greenhouse, for the Hitherto Disinclined

Some gardeners take to plant propagation like ducks to water. Natural nurturers, they live with a constant array of little pots of this and that littered around on every available hard surface, outside and in. Infuriatingly for the rest of us, all they seem to have to do to create a myriad of cuttings is to poke lifeless stumps of haphazard prunings and trimmings into pots of ropey old soil and, hey presto, the next minute – trees. Worse still, they propagate plants successfully on cluttered kitchen windowsills in algae-filled jam jars that look like the dippings from primordial swamps. There seems to be no stopping these people, except that they tend already to have completely stuffed gardens with nowhere to display the results of their over-developed talents. So what do they do? They press their ugly little charges into our hands. And *we* kill them.

This chapter is about laid-back propagation for normal mortals, for the average, busy 'killer gardeners' who have as yet to manage to grow even a broad bean in a jam jar successfully (remember school?), but who hanker after a few old-fashioned sweet peas, perhaps, or would like to take a cutting of a friend's unusual pelargonium, or maybe who need to divide a huge clump of something ordinary that has got a bit big in the border. So, no mist propagation systems, no greenhouse sterilization, no greenhouse even. No leaf cuttings of horrid African violets (shouldn't that be vile-ets?). No growing rare and temperamental orchids from seed. Just very basic propagation, getting a few new plants for nothing.

Plant Division

This is the simplest way to increase your stock of plants, and provides 'swapping material' with which to ply other gardeners. It is simplicity itself, particularly with clump-forming herbaceous perennials, such as herbaceous geraniums, all those vigorous border daisies, ornamental grasses and so on. If a plant gets too big for its boots, and preferably before it begins to weaken in the middle as a result, you dig it up and divide it into smaller sections one of which can be replanted at the original site, and the rest can be planted elsewhere or potted up and given away.

If you are dividing a really old clump, throw away the middle section and just keep the outer edge growth. As long as there is a healthy bit of root and a healthy shoot or two on each piece you retain, everything will be fine. Replant, adding plenty of organic stuff to the soil to give the new plantlets a fresh start. If you are potting up bits for friends, it goes down well and looks a bit more professional if you plant them in some decent soil-based compost such as John Innes No. 2 or 3 rather than your own garden soil, which will inevitably sprout a large population of weedlings as soon as your back is turned, thereby damaging your reputation as a real gardener.

I have been frequently amused by the number of gardening writers who assume that we all have two garden forks to insert neatly back to back into the middle of overgrown clumps of plants in order to divide them. I am sure this is the ideal way to tease apart massive roots systems if, in addition to posessing two forks, you also have five-foot-long arms and biceps like a shot-putter. In reality, for most of us, dividing large herbaceous clumps involves just one fork, one welly, an inelegant manual tussle and some doubtful language. Some smaller plants such as primulas, which have fibrous roots, can be relatively easily teased apart by hand, the separate new plantlets being quite obvious. Others seem to have steel girders built into their roots, and plants such as hostas or day lilies have to be divided by being chopped quite savagely with a spade or, for the more lily-livered amongst us, cut up using an old bread knife perhaps.

The refinement of this job is knowing what prefers to be divided when. Early autumn and spring are the traditional times for the division of clumps, but some plants react adversely if divided just before the winter. The afore-mentioned primulas will be happy if they are divided in the autumn, while those chopped up hostas will grow away more quickly if they are divided in spring when their nose-like shoots are just about to push up through the soil. As a general rule, I feel more comfortable about dividing in the spring those herbaceous plants that totally disappear underground during deepest winter. You are less likely to forget where they are if you replant them just as they are about to shoot upwards. Plants that that do not die back completely, maintaining their presence by keeping a rosette of leaves or some other evidence of life during the winter, I am happy to divide in the autumn. Of course, it all depends on the circumstances. If you are doing major work to an entire border, you just have to get on with dividing things up and replanting whatever time of they year it is and hope for the best. The moral of the tale is that you should always put marker sticks or labels into the soil where you replant things. We all think we will remember where things are, but in the hurly burly of our thrilling gardening lives, we usually forget.

Some herbaceous plants, instead of making larger and larger clumps, start to run around the border by sending out suckers. These suckers are often thought to be seedlings but, in fact, are joined to the original plant by long roots. In the main, suckers are an utter nuisance (think of garden mint) and, if they are not checked, can turn a carefully planned mixed border into mixed wilderness in a couple of seasons. However, you can sever a few suckers and pot them up to give away to your worst enemy. Conversely, I should look sideways, if I were you, at any 'friend' who offers you *Achillea ptarmica* 'The Pearl' or *Artemesia pontica* (try growing this one in a pot, which is how it looks best).

Suckers can very occasionally be fun. In my old garden I enjoyed a great on/off affair with that Colossus of the border, *Maclayea cordata*, with its man-sized stems and huge glaucous leaves. My neighbour and I sent it to and fro under our fence between our gardens for several years. One year she had it, the following year she would wage war on it and what was left would run next door to me. The next year, I would do the same, and so it went on.

Other border plants and ground cover plants spread by means of runners (like strawberry plants), new little plants being produced from a bud at the end of each shoot. All you need to do is peg the shoot down in a little pot of compost sunk into the ground near the 'mother' plant. When the new plant is produced, you can sever the shoot and you have a small potted plant to grow on, give away or plant somewhere else.

All sorts of plants can be divided: irises – the ones with the ugly, gnarled rhizomes that look like old gardeners fingers – *must* be divided and replanted if they have become congested and have stopped flowering well, and this s best done around July. You have to dig up the entire clump, throw away the worst, unproductive bit in the middle, and keep the outermost 'fingers', each with a root end and a shoot end. Replant these almost horizontally (sprinkle some bonemeal on the new site first) without covering them with soil, about 9in apart, with the shoot end to the north of the root end. This is not as barmy as it sounds – the rhizomes need full summer sun to form the next year's flower bud, so they must not be shaded by their own leaves to any great extent. Make sure therefore that the new site is really sunny.

Bulbs (daffodils, tulips, alliums) and corms (crocus, crocosmia) can be divided to increase your stock – or if they are very congested. But here, risking the wrath of the parsimonious, I tend to draw the line. Unless the bulbs or corms in question are, for example, the only specimens in the northern hemisphere and were brought back from a remote corner of the Transvaal by a famous gardener in his or her spongebag as a special, special present, then I would not bother. If you remove the small bulbs, called offsets, that you often see attached to daffodils bulbs, they will not flower for a year or two, so if you want more daffodils it is probably easier and quicker to go and buy some. If bulbs or corms stop being productive it may be that it is their growing conditions (lack of light or water), not merely congestion, that is the cause of the problem. It might be better to heave them out and start again somewhere else. Most bulbs and corms – sold loose or in packets – cost considerably less for a good few than does a bunch of flowers. If they are so very expensive, should you be spending that much anyway on a bulb, which is a pretty vulnerable and chancy form of plant life in the hands of the average gardener, however zealous? And if you disagree, go and read a proper detailed propagation book which will perhaps convince you that there are some things – such as dividing bulbs, growing shrubs, trees, or things like agapanthus or wisteria from seed – that are just not worth the effort for normal mortals. Which brings me on to…

Growing From Seed indoors

This is an area that can provide us with a lot more fun than the rather worthy and sensible area of plant division. You can grow yourself all sorts of little flights of fancy on even the slimmest of windowsills if you are of a mind to do so, if you read the instructions on the seed packets and follow some very simple rules.

You can, of course, grow perennials and biennials from seed indoors, planting them out when they are small and watching them carefully as young transplants until they mature. If you are a true beginner, however, I think it helps to start with large seeds of annuals to give you as near to instant gratification as you can get from propagation. You can just plant two or three seeds to a pot, cover them with a bit of cling film until germination, and keep an eye on them for the first weeks or so until they make their first true leaves (the ones that resemble their adult leaves). You will need to thin the seedlings down to one per pot by taking out the puniest a few weeks before you plant them out with, therefore, minimal root disturbance. The plants I usually recommend to first-time seed growers are quick annual climbers because, being large, the seeds are easy to handle, and you get a lot of growth and flower drama for the amount of effort you put in. I particularly recommend *Cobaea scandens*, canary creeper and other nasturtiums, morning glory, or some of the more interesting sweet peas, since the seedlings of these that you can buy 'off the peg' from virtually every flower shop or greengrocer you pass in early spring are invariably ordinary varieties. I have had great success growing annual climbers in fibre growing tubes, packed tightly side by side in old 2-litre plastic pots and filled with John Innes No. 1 compost. The advantage of these tubes, which are quite cheap to buy, is that they are tall and slim, encouraging deep rooting. Being biodegradable, the whole caboodle is planted in the soil and there is therefore virtually no check to the young plant's growth.

I cannot stress enough the need to hold off as long as possible on the planting of seeds indoors, where the atmosphere is dry and warm and the daylight on offer less than full, even on a windowsill. Climbers grow like the wind once they get going, and can soon outgrow any pathetic support you may have to give them (knitting needles and kebab sticks have both been spotted not a million miles from here) before the weather is genuinely warm enough for them to be planted outside so they can ramp away unchecked.

If you are more confident and a bit more ambitious, you could try to grow herbs such as coriander or basil – which you will have to sow at intervals during the summer since they go to seed or get eaten very quickly. Or you could try some big annuals such as cosmos, cleome and *Nicotiana affinis* (big white tobacco plants) mentioned earlier. Some of these present little problem since the seeds are quite manageable, and you can plant them two or three to a pot or growing tube and thin them out. Nicotiana is a different story. The seeds are like dust, and it is well nigh impossible to sow them thinly. The answer is to mix them with a little fine dry sand – sandpit sand will do – which not only 'dilutes' them, but also makes it possible to see where you have sprinkled them. All the same they will be very congested when they come up and will have to be ruthlessly culled unless you want to end up with every windowsill in the house covered with sad, stringy, lolling seedlings in little pots which need watering at least twice a day.

Guidelines for Growing from Seed Indoors Without a Greenhouse

1 The most important rule of all: don't grow too much of one thing. 'Pricking out' – the official term for thinning – dozens of seedlings like they do in proper greenhouses is for serious gardeners. It is far, far, easier to sow little potfuls of things, with just a few seeds in each. Thin out ruthlessly and chuck seedlings away if you germinate too many.

2 Use fibre pots packed in old plant pots, or special propagation packs: clear plastic domes over trays with individual cells in which to plant seeds, which make handling the plants simpler. Some propagators are sold that are windowsill shaped – longer and narrower.

3 If possible, use proper seed-growing compost – I use John Innes No. 1. Others swear by the so-called multipurpose composts, or even use the compost from Grobags. Make sure that whatever you use has had all the lumps rubbed out of it so that it has a fine texture, and that it is well saturated and drained *before* you sow your seeds. You could drench the compost with a fungicide to prevent the seedlings going mouldy (known as 'damping off') in the early days.

4 Sow seeds as thinly as possible on the damp compost and cover them with dry compost. Big seeds with hard cases, such as morning glory, should be soaked overnight beforehand. Remember that seeds need to be covered by their own 'height' of soil. Half-inch seeds need half an inch of compost on top, grains-of-sand-sized seeds need the merest sprinkling of compost on top. Do not water the pots again until the seeds have germinated or the seeds may get washed about.

5 If you are not using a little propagator, cover the pots of seed with cling film until germination. *Keep them out of the sun.*

6 Once the seeds have germinated, remove the cling film or open the vents on the propagator lid. Seedlings need a lot of light, which is where the problems start. The seedlings will get tall and skinny if they get too little light, and may dry out and die if they get too hot. If they are still in a covered propagator, they can easily get too warm and damp, and then go mouldy. You have to check on them at least once a day to make sure that all is well.

7 If you are growing a few seeds in each pot, remove the weakest ones to allow the big ones to expand, and eventually separate the two or three biggest and grow them in individual pots in stronger compost, such as John Innes No. 2.

8 When you have to handle seedlings in order to transfer them to bigger pots, pick them up by their leaves, not their stems, and use a kitchen fork to loosen their roots. Make a wide hole in the new compost pot with a pencil end, lower the delicate little roots in very carefully and water in with a few drops of water. Once transplanted, seedlings will take several days to get over the shock and start growing again.

9 Harden off young plants properly by giving them a gentle transition into the outside world. Put them outside, out of the sun and wind at first, during the day and bring them in at night for a week or so. Spring may appear to have sprung and the daytime temperatures may be quite high, but for these little chaps it is night-time temperature and soil temperature that are of crucial importance. If you take little plants off a windowsill and plunge them into the cold ground without this period of acclimatization, not only will the new leaves go very pale and be unable to grow, but the existing flimsy leaves, unused to direct sunlight, will probably scorch. Either way, you could find you have wasted a lot of time and energy.

Growing Annuals from Seed Outdoors

At some time or other in our gardening past, we have most of us succumbed to the fantasy that you can chuck a few seeds on bare earth and get miraculous results. Indeed you frequently see packets and cartons of seeds on the market tantalisingly called things like 'Cottage Garden Mixture', 'Butterfly Mixture', 'Scented Garden Mixture' that overtly tempt us into this method of gardening. The problem with growing things from seed outside is that few of us have anything like weed-free soil, and this alone makes it difficult to avoid ending up nurturing a small patch of mixed weeds until it is, humiliatingly, too late.

I am afraid the answer to this problem would seem to be to shun all the glamorously named seed mixtures and to sow patches of one thing clearly marked with little name labels, and to grow things in strict rows which is (something weeds conveniently never do). To sow, you make little channels called drills with the end of a stick. Dribble a little water along the bottom of each drill, space the seed out along them and flick the dry soil back into the drill over the seeds. Do not plant the seeds too deeply (see guideline no. 4, above), and keep the area moist once the seedlings appear by watering with a very fine rose on a watering can. If you have a cat, cover the area loosely with a small piece of chicken wire since all cats will naturally assume that a smooth piece of soil has been created especially for them to sleep in, or worse. Once the seeds have all come through the soil, start thinning them out so that they have room to grow. Don't even think about transplanting the thinnings, it just doesn't work. The eventual spacing of the plants will be indicated on the seed packet. If you don't thin out your seedlings in accordance with the instructions, you will get small and overcrowded plants that will not do very well. In my own experience it is this failure to thin seedlings out that is responsible for the greatest failures in this method of growing from seed.

Only at the behest of a television producer have I ever planted one of those borders consisting almost *entirely* of annuals, where you mark out areas with lines of sand, planting different seeds in each patch. This is just not my personal style of gardening, since it involves far too much bare earth and far too much fiddling around in late spring. It does work after a fashion, but to prevent such a volume of juicy annual growth collapsing in a rainstorm and becoming a complete mess, you need to be able to get into it and provide some sticks-and-string support, which is extremely difficult to do. And again, you run the risk of ending up with a large colony of willowherb or sow thistle suddenly flowering gamely just beyond your reach in the middle of it all. At the end of the season you have to pull it all up. You are thus back to square one again with all that naked soil, and you have very little to show for all the effort you put in. To my mind this is not good for morale. Alas, there is a vast difference between what looks good on television and what makes for satisfying gardening in real life.

Sowing Hardy Annuals and Biennials Outside in Late Summer

Most of the plants we grow as bedding plants will not self-seed in our climate, with its short growing season. I have in recent years had unexpected appearances late in the summer of self-sown tobacco plants, lobelia and even busy Lizzie but it is not something you can take for granted. However, if left to their own devices, certain annuals known as 'hardy annuals' will deposit their seeds around in late summer when they will instantly germinate, survive as small seedlings through all but the most atrocious of winters, growing on and flowering early in the following summer. In my garden I have colonies of such great border stand-bys as blue love-in-the-mist (*Nigella*), and 'Mother of Pearl' poppies (also known as 'Fairy Wings') and the currently fashionable inky-blue *Cerinthe major*, all of which survive on this basis and are invaluable.

You can start off a self-perpetuating colony by imitating nature and sowing seeds of hardy annuals randomly in a border in August or September. As long as you teach yourself to recognize the seedlings, you will get results the following summer. Even if you don't do so at first, and inadvertently weed some of them out or disturb them, some seedlings are bound to escape your ignorant rampaging and will prosper – probably in the most unlikely places, and with interesting results.

The following spring the foliage of these junior hardy annuals should be stout enough to be recognizable as something important (love-in-the-mist is distinctively feathery and quite unweedlike), so you can thin them out or isolate them into good-sized clumps. The thinnings can be re-planted, but they will not grow as big and gutsy as the undisturbed plants, and will flower later. You should dead-head these hardy annuals sparingly, just enough to encourage continued flowering. It is no great hardship to live with the old flowers – the seedheads of my love-in-the-mist and poppies have a charm of their own. With a bit of luck they will self-seed year after year. This is just the sort of gardening I love.

Biennial seeds can be cast around in midsummer in the hope that some of them will imitate nature and turn up as viable plantlets the following year, to flower two summers hence. In my experience, sowing biennials this way is a bit of a long shot, as the likelihood of person-sown seed falling on suitable ground and coming through two seasons without mishap is slim. I am thinking here particularly of foxgloves, whose dust-like seeds and miniscule seedlings seemed to have had a distinct preference for germinating only between two paving stones in the middle of an important thoroughfare in my old garden. The same plant is a certifiably lunatic weed in my new garden. Honesty seed is chunkier and has more of a chance of sensible success, and is therefore worth a try. The answer is to sow biennials in groups in specific places. Since they transplant well after their first year's growth, they can be re-located and shoe-horned into odd corners around the garden to look 'natural'. This bit of well-planned artifice is practised by numerous gardeners, and works a treat.

Shrub Propagation – Layering and Taking Cuttings

To many gardeners, taking cuttings is what proper propagation is all about. It seems to be a matter of taking on the challenge of persuading by various means all sorts of plants to produce roots from unexpected places, stems or sometimes shoot-tips, or even leaves.

My own success with cuttings is, I freely admit, patchy, and my excuses vary depending on how defensive I feel about it. Generally I claim that my lack of zeal and/or success has a lot to do with the fact that for most of my gardening life I have been a gardener with an exceedingly stuffed small garden, offering me little incentive to take cuttings of shrubs. Also, when I started out I had keen gardener parents who pressed their surplus cuttings in to my ever-open hands. I had, as so often is the case, a crowded sill-less centrally heated house, making it hard to succeed with anything that needed protection from the elements. When I tried things out, I attempted to do everything 'right' and yet still ended up with half a dozen cuttings of something I frankly didn't need or very much like while the things I was really desperate to acquire died on me if I so much as took my eyes off them. I feel instinctively that I am fairly typical of today's keen but pampered gardeners.

I will, therefore, outline the principles behind the fairly complex subject of layering and taking stem cuttings. Whether or not you turn out to be a natural taker-of-cuttings is, I am convinced, in the lap of the gods.

Most of us will have noticed, in the course of grubbing about on our hands and knees tidying up under shrubs, that branches touching the ground often spontaneously put out roots and attach themselves to the soil. This is a shrub's natural way of propagating itself and illustrates to us gardeners the basic magic behind it all. The roots, as you will have noticed, are produced from around the point where a leaf joins a stem, called a node. Plants such as ivy (which, after all, is a shrubby climber) produce roots and shoots from just about every node that touches the ground, and special clinging roots where it touches rough, climbable surfaces.

Using a technique known as **layering**, you can persuade all sorts of shrubs to produce roots on branches still attached to themselves by making a small cut behind a node and pegging the branch down on to the ground each side of the cut. The soil in the immediate area can be improved with a little good compost to ensure that it retains moisture. It is a good idea to pinch out the tip of the branch, to stop it putting its energy into growing. Whilst slow-growing plants such as rhododendrons will take a year to get going, some shrubs put down roots this way fairly quickly: if you carry out the operation in the spring, by the end of the summer the roots should have started to grow and you can then sever the new (rather odd-shaped) plant from its 'mother'. Minimize the shock by leaving it undisturbed until the following spring, after which time it can be regarded as an independent new plant, and transplanted with care in a new site. This is probably the easiest way to propagate a wide variety of shrubs, and it is certainly worth having a go. I have even cut and pegged down branches of friend's shrubs – with their permission – and made them into surrogate propagators for me. It was very satisfying and I had far greater success with layering than I did taking proper hardwood cuttings (see below) in my overcrowded little patch.

Perhaps at this point I will slip in a little about propagating shrubs from suckers. I refer to shrubs such as stag's horn sumach (*Rhus typhina*). The principle of severing a shoot from the mother plant, leaving it in situ while it makes its own roots and moving it a few weeks or months later is similar to layering, in that you have to persuade a part of the original plant to make itself into an independent plant. In the case of suckers, however, you have to sever the plant from its parent first, in order to force it to make its new roots, and it is really important that you do not disturb the sucker for several months afterwards or it will just wither and die. Sumach suckers wildly, and is often regarded as a weed. However, the female, with its scarlet autumn tints and russet cone-like flowers that last well in to the winter, is a wonderful plant, and worth all the bother of eliminating its unwanted suckers. You can only be sure of acquiring a female, of course, by taking a sucker from a female. In my experience, you rarely find female sumachs in garden centres and nurseries – you have generally to take pot luck as to their sex.

If you take suckers from shrubs that have been grafted, you will end up with a wild plant. (See the section on rose suckers, page 108.)

The most common way to propagate shrubs and many other plants is, however, by taking **stem cuttings**, forcing the plant to produce roots from shoots cut from them at various stages of development. As with layering, the roots are produced from the most active growing point on the stem, just below a node. Most cuttings are thus what are known as 'nodal' cuttings. However, many shrubs also respond well to what are known as 'heel cuttings', where a side shoot is torn gently from a main stem, the resulting pointed shred of bark from the main stem is trimmed neatly, and the shoot inserted into compost. Handbooks on the subject of propagation detail which shrubs respond best to each method, and if you are going into the whole propagation thing seriously you will need more information than I can provide here.

If you are fortunate enough to have an unused patch of ground that is sheltered, shaded at mid-day and not dry (not under trees, for example), you can dig in a little sand and compost to improve the soil texture and make a small cuttings bed to take **hardwood cuttings** of shrubs which are the slowest, but easiest, to handle.

At the end of the growing season, you should cut shoots about 30cm long from fairly stiff and brownish wood (often referred to as 'mature') that was formed in that current year. Cuts should be cleanly made just below a node, and the shoots, having had their lower leaves removed, should be stuck in the soil to the depth of about 15cm. You should reckon on about a 30 per cent success rate, so you should take at least six cuttings of any one variety. They will do absolutely nothing until well into the next spring and you will be convinced, by about April, that you are nurturing a graveyard. But you must absolutely resist the temptation to poke around or tweak at the little row of corpses to see if they have got roots. I write as one who knows, having impatiently pulled up many a shrivelled, perished looking bit of vegetation only to discover little roots at the bottom. Alas, even if you shove them straight back and pretend you didn't do anything, they invariably die. Patience should be rewarded when some, not all, of the undisturbed little twigs start to sprout new leaves. Make sure they do not dry out during the following growing season, and by the autumn you will have some free, albeit small, new plants. They are best left where they are until the spring, when they can be moved to their new homes.

While **hardwood cuttings** are not generally taxing or time consuming, needing only an extraordinary degree of patience, a square metre or so of appropriately sited soil and a philosophical attitude towards failure, **semi-hardwood cuttings** are a completely different cup of tea. Whatever anyone else says or writes about the subject, I must insist that it is really difficult to propagate from semi-hardwood cuttings without a) serious dedication, b) a greenhouse or a proper cold frame and c) a singular lack of desire or need for a summer holiday away from home. I cannot recommend this method of propagation to all but the fanatical few. Having stated all that, if it turns out that you are one of the lucky ones for whom any form of propagation is as simple as falling of a log, you can feel really smug.

Semi-hardwood cuttings can be taken, as the name suggests, from half-ripened (i.e. quite bendy and green), non-flowering side shoots from the current season's growth from a large variety of shrubs, generally in mid- to late-summer. They root very quickly, in a matter of weeks, provided they are kept constantly humid but shaded, in a greenhouse or cold frame outdoors. Cuttings should be about 10cm long, with a straight cut just below a node and lower leaves removed. Lavender and rosemary seem to do better if they are taken as heel cuttings as described briefly above. They should be inserted into pots of John Innes no.1 or a mixture of sand and peat that will provide both moisture retention and good drainage. The method of taking the cuttings is very similar to the softwood cuttings described below. The big enemies are overheating, and the development of mould in the humid conditions, which rapidly kills the cuttings before they have a chance to root. You can replicate the conditions of a warm, humid greenhouse by enclosing the pots of cuttings in various ways (described below), drenching the pots with a fungicide such as Cheshunt compound and making sure that the leaves of the shoots do not touch the sides of whatever it is you have used to cover them. You should stand the pots outside in the shade, gradually reducing the humidity by puncturing holes in the bag as the cuttings makes roots. I have succeeded on a few occasions with fuchsias using this method, but as often as not everything goes black and furry with mould after a week or so. A further slight discouragement arises from the fact that within a few weeks of having been put into compost, and having been the centre of so much attention and worry, the little cuttings will drop their leaves with the natural arrival of autumn. There may be no further sign of life until the spring, by which time, if you are anything like me, you will probably have lost interest in them anyway.

I feel bad that I am passing on so much negativity about semi-hardwood cuttings, when I know that success is largely about having the right equipment and just a bit of luck.

Perhaps we should look at something a little easier: **softwood cuttings**. This is the name given to stem cuttings that are taken from young shoots that have not become hard or woody, and is the method used for propagating pelargoniums (often wrongly called geraniums), argyranthemums (frequently called marguerites) and a lot of the half-hardy perennials that we grow in containers. If you have a yen to try stem cuttings and you don't have space for a cuttings bed, a cold frame or a greenhouse with all the expensive gadgets and gizmos that 'pukka' gardeners have, then you should have a go at this.

Cuttings should be between 5 and 10cm long and taken from soft fleshy main or side shoots. I find it best to cut off an entire shoot first and then take a series of cuttings from it using a craft knife and a chopping board. You can take three or four cuttings from one shoot, cutting neatly just below each leaf joint. All you need is a piece of a stem that has a node with a neat cut beneath it – each cutting does not need to have a growing tip. Pelargoniums, in particular, are very vigorous plants and you can take cuttings from them at virtually any time during the growing season. It makes sense to make a few cuttings from the shoots you remove when you cut back the lanky plants that you have over-wintered indoors in February. It also makes sense to take a few cuttings at the end of summer from those in pots outdoors that are too big to move into shelter, but will probably get nipped by a frost.

Experienced gardeners invariably find their own ways of taking softwood cuttings, and every one will swear that their method is foolproof. A friend always (successfully, of course) takes masses of softwood cuttings in supermarket meat trays filled with damp vermiculite and covered in clingfilm, or simply wedges part of a polystyrene tile into an ice-cream carton filled in water, makes holes in it and pokes little stems through them into the water. She is definitely 'one of those'. Perhaps, however, I should outline the 'text book' version for beginners:

Fill a 2-litre plastic pot with John Innes No. 1 and make sure it is well drenched with a solution of a fungicide. Dip the cuttings in the same solution, and also dip the ends into some hormone rooting powder to help with the formation of the roots, before inserting them into the compost, about four to a pot. A propagator makes life easier, or failing that, you should make what are known as Wisley cloches for individual pots of cuttings. (The cuttings are sealed inside little tents made out of clear plastic bags supported and kept away from the leaves by a couple of wire hoops inserted into the pots, as shown.) Another way of making sure the cuttings stay humid is to make a 'hat' for the pot out of the top half of a clear plastic drinks bottle (with the lid on it, initially).

The cuttings should be kept out of the sun, and the humidity level kept high until evidence of root growth appears (that is, tiny leaves on the shoot). During this time the propagators or cloches will become completely steamed up, which is fine. If they are in Wisley cloches, you then reduce the humidity by cutting the corner off the plastic bag but leaving it in place for a further week or two. If they are in a plastic propagator, you can open the vent in the lid. The screw top of the drinks bottle cloche can conveniently be removed. Once the cuttings are established (two to five weeks or so, depending on the time of year) they should be potted on to a growing medium with a bit more oomph to it, such as John Innes No. 2, and feeding should start.

There is more, much more, to propagating your own plants than I have outlined here, as you will see from even the most cursory glance at a book on the subject. I have not mentioned basal cuttings, leaf cuttings, eye cuttings, root cuttings, Irishman's cuttings, grafting, and heaven knows what else. But there should be enough here to get you started. If you still think it is all rather complicated and irrelevant, next time you accidentally snap a shoot off a fuchsia or a busy Lizzie, stick it in jar of water and see what happens. Before you know it you may find you have joined the Primordial Swamp Mob, and life may never be quite the same again.

CHAPTER 10

La Batterie du Jardin — Some Tools You Seriously Need, and Some You Seriously Do Not

I write this section in response to two things. Firstly, as a rookie gardener I remember I made several mistakes and bought some useless tools. In an attempt to save money, I undoubtedly wasted a lot. Secondly, I am asked often by visitors to my garden and by my students to recommend tools that I have found indispensable. There are so many tools and gadgets on display in most garden centres that it is genuinely hard to take decisions and to sort out priorities, especially if you have never bought things for the garden before. It is the same with all tools, and is symptomatic of the times in which we live. Only if you go to a good old-fashioned hardware shop to buy a saw or a screwdriver, or even a power drill, will you find someone behind the counter who has enough personal experience and know-how to point you in the right direction. The trouble with the huge garden centres and DIY superstores, where most of the gardening stuff is bought, is that there is no one there to help in quite the same way.

The difficulty in writing about tools is, of course, that they are very personal. Something that I find invaluable could be useless to someone else. Obviously, I have not tried every gadget and gizmo on the market. I will do my best to list tools I think would be useful to the majority of gardeners.

Spades and forks

I hardly need say that everyone needs a spade and fork. The question is what sort.

Firstly I would say that they must be stainless steel. Once you have used stainless steel digging tools you will understand why. They cut well, they are lighter, they don't get clogged up and heavy, except occasionally in the most appalling Wadhurst clay (which is as bad as you can get, I assure you). They are more expensive than ordinary metal ones, but they are a lot cheaper than they used to be.

For years I used a small spade – bought for me as a birthday present doubtless because I am a small female person and it was deemed appropriate. Also, I had a small garden, with small borders, and everything was done on a fairly small scale. I have recently started using a bigger spade. The lightness of the stainless steel means that it is not noticeably harder work to use, and when there is a large quantity of straightforward digging to do, it is definitely quicker. The small one is still brought into service for little jobs.

I still use my original small 'border' fork – a standard-sized one feels unwieldy and you can't get it in to tight corners.

I would like to say stainless steel forks are indestructible – mine, however, has had a bent tine for about ten years. I lent it to a rather large and enthusiastic New Zealander, and I think the combination of his bulk and a large underground rock got the better of it. Perhaps I should have complained to the manufacturer, but I bet there was something in the small print on the guarantee about the size of both New Zealanders and rocks. It is too late now, anyway.

Trowels and hand-forks

Again, I am sure it comes as no surprise to hear that these are totally essential, and if you have a large garden, you probably need more than one of each – one to use and one to lose. You might imagine that you can manage with just a trowel, but you really do need a small fork as well since a fork makes hand-weeding so much easier.

I am afraid they have to be stainless steel again, since nothing else quite cuts the mustard. You can pay a lot or a little, depending on the type of steel, no doubt, and the type of handle. The most important thing about a trowel, particularly, is that it feels well balanced in your hand, so play around with a few before you buy. My personal favourite has quite a long (2½in) crooked shank between the blade and the handle, which is wooden. I find that my shankless, stubbier and substantially cheaper one, while it is a nice weight and very strong, is a little short over all and therefore a bit limiting. I have learnt to be a bit wary of wooden handles. If they are a tasteful unflashy horticultural brown, you lose them in the garden on their first day out. If they are the bright varnished ones, the varnish peels off and can be uncomfortable in the hand, or worse, the metal part of the tool can actually come lose as the wood swells.

I have never managed to get on well with trowels and hand forks with much longer (over 35cm) handles. In principal the idea is great, but I find them too exhausting to use. Nor do I like those hand tools with removable handles, or should they be described as handles with removable tools? All a bit too fussy for the likes of me.

Incidentally, brightly coloured PVC tape wrapped round the handles of small discreetly coloured garden tools makes them easier to see, and makes them less likely to end up at the bottom of the compost heap.

There are all sorts of wonder hand-tools on the market for this or that, designed to take the hard graft out of all manner of garden drudgery. I have never managed to get on very well with weed removers, bulb planters and the like, so perhaps the advice is to try out someone else's gizmos before you buy. I have a strong suspicion that all the truly useful garden tools have already been invented, but I try not to have a closed mind about it.

Long-handled forks

These are small forks – the business end is about the same size as the hand-fork above – but with very long handles. The one I have had for years is about a metre long overall has a very 1970's 'avocado' handle and is incredibly lightweight. I have seen other versions that are heavier than mine, with wider tines, and they were not nearly as easy to use. Long-handled forks are invaluable for those of us with stuffed borders with minimal access, for twiddling the surface of the soil to de-compact it, to dislodge weeds that are out of reach, or to 'fiddle in' fertilizers to the top few inches of soil, using just a twist of the wrist. This is one of my most valued tools, and I cannot imagine gardening without it.

Hoes

For some reason – memories of Mr. McGregor, or our grandfathers, in well-tended vegetable gardens, perhaps – we all think we need one of these. I have to say, that after twenty or so years gardening, I have only just acquired one, simply because I have only just started to grow things (namely vegetables) in rows that you can hoe between. The function of a hoe is to dislodge or decapitate weeds between rows of vegetables without disturbing the soil too much thereby activating another generation of dormant weed-seeds. So in overstuffed flower gardens, you don't have much use for a hoe. I am now the proud owner of a rather neat little wedge-shaped gadget called a Swoe, which I love.

Rakes

Rakes also belong in the vegetable garden, but have more general use in the garden, for smoothing out and tidying up areas with lumpy soil. You should never use an ordinary rake on the lawn, however, or you will rip the turf to bits.

Lawn rakes

I have always found this an indispensable tool, even when I only had a small lawn. You need to rake out the debris and dead grass from lawns in the autumn and again, more gently, in the spring. Lawn rakes are also useful for raking up leaves and other rubbish from gravel areas. My favourite has plastic tines and is bright turquoise blue. The traditional metal ones bend out of shape very quickly, I find.

Secateurs

With secateurs, you get what you pay for. I have two pairs of very posh red-handled ones, which are the Rolls Royces of secateurs and wonderful to use. I reserve these for proper pruning and keep them in leather holsters and wipe them with lubricants every so often. Then I have other ones which have seen betters days, been left outside by mistake, spent time abandoned on garden walls and so on, and have definitely dropped into the second or third division. I cut just about anything and everything with these and I love them to bits.

I have recently lost another pair that I found extremely useful. I bought them at Hampton Court Flower Show and, as I recall, they were Canadian. They had a ratchet in the handle, which made cutting over-large branches extremely easy. They were cheap, visible (bright yellow and green) and lightweight, and I hope they turn up soon because I miss them.

I have to say that there is an awful lot of snobbery and 'posery' attached to the choice of secateurs. If you don't do much pruning, and always find yourself cutting garden wire with your secateurs, then don't buy a £40 pair just because everyone says they are the best. You neither need (nor deserve) the best, do you?

Kitchen/garden scissors

I have several pairs of rough, tough, cheap (under £2 a pair) scissors that I could not do without which I buy from a mail-order kitchen-supply company. I do everything from opening fertilizer bags and dead-heading to cutting wire with them. They are dark blue and dark green, unfortunately, so they are frequently mislaid. Perhaps I should try to persuade the company to make them in bright yellow for dippy gardeners.

Loppers and pruners

Two-handled pruners are a boon if you have trees and climbers that need constant attention. Judging by the number of people that have borrowed mine, they are clearly something that is not seen as a priority purchase, but I think it should be. The ones I find the easiest to use have handles around 60cm long. I find that a pair with telescopic handles is too unwieldy when extended, and too heavy when in short mode. My advice is to buy the lightest you can find, since trimming overhead branches is tiring even for the toughest of us.

A useful tree-pruning gadget (also borrowed by neighbours) is my 'parrot beak' pruner on a telescopic pole. It has a saw attachment which is also much in demand. Nearly everyone has overhanging trees and unreachable climbers and this really does make a difference to the chore of trying to keep them in check. In my view it is worth every penny. Now I have moved away, I expect that nearly every gardener in my old street has had to go out and buy one – my heart bleeds.

Small pruning saw

I have a wonderful, small, folding pruning saw with a red handle, that is indispensable. It is particularly useful for getting between the thick lower stems of old roses you could not possibly cut with secateurs. Pruning saws are incredibly sharp – potentially lethal, in fact – with a row of teeth that makes 'Jaws' look like something from a toothpaste ad. It makes sense *not* to own one that cannot be folded away, especially if there are children in the household.

Garden knife

I have been given several garden knives in my time – indeed, it would seem to be the ideal small present for a keen gardener. My knives were natty little folding things. One of them, as I remember, even had a beautiful polished wooden handle with brass bits on it. I am ashamed to say that I have never used a garden knife, however, because I am not at all sure what they are actually for. The sort of pruning and propagating I do doesn't require the services of a knife, and for cutting twine I carry my beloved scissors or old secateurs with me most of the time I am out and about in my garden. I have tried hard to find a use for a garden knife. On several occasions I have slipped one into a waistcoat pocket at the start of a gardening marathon, feeling very Geoff Hamilton and very proper, but have failed to find any use for it whatsoever all day. All my knives have somehow or other vanished now, probably to the great compost heap in the sky, and I doubt if I shall replace them.

Besom (witch's broom)

Now here is a tool no gardener should be without. It is cheap too. Besoms are invaluable for sweeping leaves off lawns, borders and rockeries without damaging other plants. I used to use mine with an ordinary sweeping action, much as you would use an ordinary broom, until I saw some old gaffer doing it properly, and sweeping leaves far more efficiently as a result. You should hold the broom down low, almost horizontal to the ground, and whisk the leaves into broad heaps. You should also acquire two small pieces of plywood with which to pick up the resulting heaps. The plastic scoopers I have come across that are sold for this purpose are all far too fiddly and impossible to use if you are wearing gloves.

Gloves

Ugh, how I hate them! In fact I don't know anyone who likes using gardening gloves. They make you so clumsy, prevent you from feeling what you are doing, and get wet, filthy and rigid with soil. And have you ever borrowed anyone else's much-used ones? I would almost rather borrow someone else's toothbrush. Yet unless you want to have hands like a navvy by the time you are thirty-five, you have to find some that will do the business. The trouble is that there are so many gardening gloves on the market, presumably to cater for every conceivable gardening need, and to fit every conceivable shape of hand. In reality, all too many of them are either made of useless and inappropriate materials for gardening or seem to have been designed to fit a curious selection of alien monsters, and definitely do not fit average women's hands.

After many years of trial and error, I think I have at last found a selection of gloves that just about copes with my various needs. I am extremely fond of my dark green **synthetic gloves** that are thornproof, softly padded and washable and have the advantage of snug-fitting cuffs (very visible lime green) that stop soil going down inside – which is important. I bought them through a gardening mail order catalogue, but I have also seen them for sale in some garden centres. Their main disadvantage is that while they are fairly water-resistant, if they do get sopping wet they are extremely unpleasant to wear. They are a also a bit too hot to use comfortably in the summer.

For dry gardening, and potting up in my tiny greenhouse, I use some little dark blue or dark green **cotton gloves** with non-slip vinyl dots printed on to the palms and fingers. They are cool to use and wash in the machine, although they shrink a little. You can buy them in most garden centres.

A couple of years ago at Hampton Court Flower Show I bought a pair of **American gloves** that looked most strange: stretchy jersey on the back, and rubber on the palm and fingers. They turned out to be supremely comfortable and incredibly efficient – just the job for messy planting and general mucking around, but, of course, being basically rubber, no good for prickly pruning. They fitted so closely that I could really feel things through them and could even tie knots and bows with them on. I used them until the fabric on the knuckles eventually wore out but, to my delight, I have recently found out that I can get replacements from a well-known mail-order fertilizer company. They could be the very thing to sort out even the most entrenched anti-glove gardeners.

Surprisingly, my favourite glove this year has been a pair of **tough red suede gloves** with a cotton lining and a strap on the wrist that tightens up with Velcro. They have moulded to the shape of my hands, are getting unspeakably shiny through so much use and now feel like part of me. In fact, they look exactly like the revolting ones I remember my mother wearing and, horror of horrors, offering to lend me when I was younger.

I have finally kicked the habit of naked-handed gardening and feel as strange without a pair of gloves on out there as I do if I accidentally start my car without my seatbelt on. All of which probably goes to show how you can become conditioned to absolutely anything in the end, and that, try as we might to resist doing so, we all end up like our mothers.

Watering cans

What on earth, you may say, can possibly be said about watering cans? *Of course* we all need one. Well, yes, we do, but there are watering cans and watering cans. In this fascinating field the French have us knocked into a cocked hat, as the expression goes.

The design of French watering cans, which have single handles that arch over from the base to the top in line with the spout, is such that you can carry and use them one with one hand. Instead of being round, as you might expect, the cans are oval in profile, so that they don't knock your legs as you walk and slop water into your slippers. As you carry them, your hand is in the same position as if you were carrying a suitcase. Your other hand is, therefore, free to carry your breakfast coffee or your pre-prandial tipple, or if the mood takes you, a pair of secateurs or a trowel.

Watering cans of the traditional two-handled British design, however, are cumbersome and cylindrical in shape, and have to be carried by the top handle with your hand unnaturally crooked forward, ape-style. When they are heavy and full, you have to hold both handles to enable you to pour from them. Anything else you are trying to carry must therefore be tucked into a pocket, held between the teeth, or put down (and lost).

I find it fascinating that such a basic bit of garden equipment should be so different – and so much better – on the other of the Channel. I thought the British were supposed to be the great gardeners. I decided to look into the matter further and unearthed the fact that at some time in the past, we and the French apparantly 'swapped' designs because we preferred each other's watering cans. What is it about our relationship with our nearest neighbour, I wonder. I am happy to say, however, that I have recently spotted plastic watering cans in the 'French' style at a very ordinary garden centre in West London. They were, of course, about twice the price of the ones I purchased a few months earlier in a French hardware store. I don't suppose many people come through customs at Gatwick Airport with a 10-litre green plastic watering can clutched firmly in each hand, but maybe this will start a trend.

You can find watering cans in hypermarkets in France. Failing that the French for hardware is *bricolage*, and a watering can is *un arrosoir*. For some inexplicable reason, the word is a masculine one!

On a more practical note, a watering can of any nationality holding more than 10 litres (which is approximately the same as two gallons) is too heavy for most of us. I find several smaller cans more useful than one large one. I also like cans with really long spouts.

On the subject of watering, I do recommend getting a hose reel for your hose. For small gardens the new automatically non-scrambling retractable ones look like a godsend if you can bear to spend so much money on such an intrinsically boring item. I have mentioned elsewhere the lance attachment that makes it so easy to water things out of reach, delivering as softly as rain water as if the hose were a watering can. I love this gadget so much that it deserves a second mention.

Mowers

If you have a lawn you need a mower and unless you sensibly decide, like my stepson, that it is crazy to acquire a noisy bit of machinery to cut a lawn the size of a face flannel when an old-fashioned push one will do, you will probably opt for an electric one. However, most men and other enthusiastic lawnists will insist on a mower that cuts really short and has a roller so that they can get 'stripes'. This is all very well if you have excellent grass and the site is very flat. It is not all very well if you have a badly lumpy lawn and you have to mow it when it is even the tiniest bit wet. The best type of mower for bad, wet grass is a rotary mower; one with a wheel at each corner, a whirring rotary blade underneath and a grass collection box. There all sorts on the market, in various sizes with all sorts of special features to make, it is claimed, your mowing life more pleasurable. You can get rotary mowers with tiny rollers on the back which will give you a bit of a stripey effect as long as you walk up and down your lawn as if you are using a proper cylinder mower (the traditional kind). I have always found, however, that for little lawns a kind of 'hoovering' action was easier to do, so the roller wasn't really significant. There are battery-powered rotary mowers (which are more expensive but mercifully quiet) and petrol-powered rotary mowers (which are noisier, but more robust and a bit more versatile). Having finally worn my little green electric rotary mower to bits – it took ten years of hard work and abuse of every kind – we have now acquired, along with masses of really awful grass, a huge, snorting, Japanese petrol-powered rotary mower that can just about cope with anything you point it at. It is a veritable off-roader with attitude and we have developed a great affection for it.

When you start measuring your garden in acres and parts thereof, it is probably time to acquire a sit-on mower. Since these should come under a general heading 'boys' toys', I would not dream of offering any opinions or advice, since I am sure they would be completely ignored.

Shears and trimmers

Ideally, you should have two kinds of shears, the long-handled type used for edging the lawn and a pair of ordinary hedge-cutting shears. If you have a really small lawn, you can just about get away with using an old pair of scissors for the lawn edge. The proper shears, however, which will not break the bank, make the job a lot quicker and save all that grovelling around. What you absolutely do not need is a half-moon lawn-edging tool. These you can borrow from someone just once a year if you really think it is necessary to tidy up your lawn edge. More frequently done than this, and you will end up with an exceedingly small lawn.

If I had unlimited time, I would always cut a small hedge by hand. There is something therapeutic about the sound of shears and satisfying about the precision and the personal contact you make with the plants as you sculpt them. You need shears anyway for all sorts of small jobs around the garden, from the mid-season trimming back of messy perennials like catmint to tidying up odd corners of grass and 'haircut' pruning of small shrubs such as potentilla. As with any tool that you use with arms extended, unless you are an Amazon, it is important to choose lightweight shears. And treat them well. Clean them and wipe them with WD40 before you put them away after each session. The sap from any hedge pruning will soon build up into a sticky, rusty coating on the blades, and they will deteriorate fast.

Urban and suburban hedge trimming with a power tool is inevitably a very obtrusive activity, second only to shredding (see below) in its anti-social nature. Battery-powered trimmers are the quietest but, if you have lots to do, it would be inconvenient to have to re-charge the battery, and power tools with fading batteries are annoying. I have an electric hedge trimmer that is wonderfully sharp and easy to use, its only limitation being the length of its flex. I can just about manage to reach what I need to do with the aid of extension leads, but a petrol-powered trimmer would probably be more practical. However, I just could not stand the noise.

When choosing a hedge trimmer, never underestimate how tiring it is to use, and chose the lightest possible for your needs. I write as one who suffers.

Shredder

Strictly speaking, all woody prunings and hedge trimmings should be snipped up into little pieces about 4cm long before they are put in a compost heap so that they will rot down properly. This involves the most tedious waste of precious gardening time, and the job is particularly irksome if you often have a large quantity of prickly stuff like pyracantha or roses to process. It was a great day for gardeners when they invented the shredder. With the aid of one of these horrendously rackety machines, all manner of garden clippings and trimmings can be reduced to about a quarter of their bulk and made into rapidly rotting chippings which, once composted, can be returned to the soil to do the utmost good.

Shredding becomes almost addictive. I have found myself scouring the garden hunting for suitable rubbish to shred, eyeing up likely branches of invasive trees and, on one occasion, even offering to shred the neighbour's prunings. Once you have got a shredder up and running, you never want to turn it off. There are various electric shredders available that are suitable for smaller gardens and you should get the most powerful that you can afford and have the space to store. Some have wheels, which makes moving them about easier. Petrol shredders make a lot of unpleasant noise, and are for larger gardens with more distant neighbours. The new 'quiet' shredders, developed in response to stringent German noise-pollution regulations, are a wonder to behold, munching discreetly with barely a murmur on pieces of wood thicker than your thumb.

Having said all this in praise of shredders, I have to admit they are not cheap and it may be a good idea to pool resources with neighbours. This way the noise-pollution problem can be a matter for mutual agreement and tolerance. On a practical note, many of the smaller shredders do not react well if stuffed with a load of soft green trimmings, or anything that is damp. Once they get clogged up, they are a bore to dismantle and clean out. Most soft greenery does not strictly need to be shredded before being added to the compost heap, but, to avoid problems, trimmings from such evergreen juicy shrubs as choisya should be shredded together with more woody branches. You should always clean a shredder properly when you have finished with it. I spray the blade with WD40 before I put it away to make sure it stays rust-free. When using a shredder, you should always wear eye protection since bits of twig frequently shoot out of the top when the blade is whizzing round, and you should also wear your stoutest gloves. It goes without saying that children should be kept well away when the shredder is in use, but I'll say it anyway.

Useful odds and ends

Essential research for this section finds me grovelling around in my less than perfectly tidy shed wishing I did all the things that I advise everyone else to do. Recognizable items retrieved from the soily gloom include the following:

Garden twine At least one ball, either green or natural coloured. (I look for 4-ply.) Twine is so often sold in those impossible old-fashioned cellophane wrappers that, once removed, reduce the ball to something resembling the regurgitation of an outsize owl that has accidentally eaten a knitting bag. The secret is never to remove the packaging, and to find the end of the string in the hole in the centre of the reel, not on the outside edge, as you would on a reel of sewing cotton. Couldn't the manufacturers of the twine supply us with cheap, unlosable bright plastic twine holders and save us all a lot of bother? Come to think of it, the way they make the twine ensures that they must sell an awful lot more than is actually used in the garden. No point in pursuing that one, then. Alternatively, you can keep the twine on a smart oak stand, like the one I bought at one of those National Trust shops that are full of tea towels and potpourri.

I use twine for just about every small tying-up job in the garden, with double or even treble thickness if the situation warrants it since it does so little harm to plant stems. You should make sure you make a couple of twists to act as a buffer between stems and the support to which you are tying them. I generally tie things up using small bows, not knots. Although the twine only lasts about a year before it has to be replaced, it is useful to have a bow you can slip undone and re-tie, since adjustments often have to be made mid-season.

Plant labels and an indelible pen Ordinary pencil wears off before your memory has time to take over.

A small hammer It is simpler to acquire one specially for the garden. You also need a bag of galvanized staples and nails.

A few plantclips A cross between a clothes peg and the things you close food bags with – very useful for keeping shoots and branches of climbers out of your way while pruning.

A roll of green plastic-covered garden wire

An assortment of bamboo canes When they get old and past it, I cut them up into short engths to use as markers for 'invisible' plants such as newly planted bulbs, and as props for 'sticks-and-string' design modifications.

A plastic measuring jug This should have the words 'garden only' written on the side with the indelible pen.

A Sussex trug /a large bendy rubber bucket with two handles Both of these are useful when weeding, and for carting things around when a barrow would be unnecessary.

A 1.25-litre pump spray bottle with a green lid I keep this one for insecticides and fungicides. Draw, in indelible pen, a large picture of a greenfly on its back with its legs in the air, since it must never be confused with the next item.

A 1.25-litre pump spray bottle with a red lid Keep this one for weedkillers. Draw a lurid skull and crossbones on it. Nothing should be left to chance.

Old kitchen knives, forks and spoons Keep these in a compartmented box, with other small items, such as labels and pens.

A green reinforced plastic sheet with handles at each corner I call this The Drag. Self-explanatory and indispensible.

One reason my little shed becomes untidy is that it is so badly lit – and I so often find myself putting away my tools at dusk. I am about to install a light, which should help.

It is definitely worth getting fundamentally organized in there, however, and I have found that the secret is hooks – many of them, at various heights and spaced at various intervals, on the shed's framework, so that you can hang up everything that can be hung to minimize floor clutter.

I have a small shelf unit against one wall. On the top shelf, in a small wicker crate so they cannot be seen, I keep my chemicals and nasties, and in another are my old knives, labels, pens, etc. (My secateurs and gloves I keep in a drawer in the house, along with scissors, a trowel and another ball of twine.)

Bags of fertilizers, once opened, each have a huge old black plant pot in which to stand so they don't fall over. As I have mentioned before, I transfer boxed soluble feeds into plastic cartons with names (and mixing quantities) marked on them with indelible marker. I used to keep packets of seed in a small wooden box in the shed – until it occured to me that the extreme heat in there in summer would damage them – so now they live in the kitchen drawer along with the other garden essentials..

Plant Lists

months = flowering time (e.g. 6–7 = June–July)

foliage + = grown chiefly for foliage but also flowers

a = annual   b = biennial   p = perennial

Herbaceous plants for a shady border – a basic list

PLANT NAME	MONTHS	TYPE
FRONT ROW		
Ajuga (foliage +)	4–9+	p
Arum italicum 'Pictum' (foliage +)	6+berries	p
Bergenia cordifolia (foliage +)	2–5+	p
Convallaria majalis	5–6	p
Dicentra formosa		
(e.g. 'Stuart Boothman')	5–9	p
Euphorbia amygdaloides 'rubra'		
(foliage +)	4–6+	p
Geranium macrorrhizum	5–7	p
Geum rivale	4–7	p
Hellebores	3–6	p
Heuchera (e.g. 'Palace Purple')	5–9	p
Hosta (foliage +)	5–9	p
Iberis sempervirens	5–6	(shrub)
Impatiens (busy Lizzie)	6–9	a
Lamium 'White Nancy', 'Beacon		
Silver', etc. (foliage +)	4–9+	p

PLANT NAME	MONTHS	TYPE
Pulmonaria (foliage +)	4–5+	p
Tellima grandiflora 'Purpurea'		
(foliage +)	5–7	p
Tiarella cordifolia	4–6	p
Tolmiea menziesii (foliage +)	4–10	p
Viola cornuta	6–7	p
Viola labradorica (foliage +)	5–7	p
SECOND ROW		
Aquilegia	5–8	p
Astrantia major	6–10	p
Crocosmia	7–8	p
Dicentra spectabilis	5–8	p
Geranium 'Wargrave Pink',		
'Phaeum', etc.	6–8	p
Lunaria annua (honesty)	5–6	b
Lunaria rediviva	6–9	p
Lysimachia punctata	6–8	p
Polygonatum (Solomon's seal)	5–6	p
Symphytum variegatum (foliage +)	6–7+	p
Tradescantia	6–9	p
THIRD ROW		
Acanthus (foliage +)	7–8+	p
Anenome japonica	7–9	p
Digitalis (foxglove)	6–7	b
Echinops	7–8	p

PLANT NAME	MONTHS	TYPE
Geranium 'Claridge Druce'	5–8	p
Lilium 'Regale', 'Pink Perfection',		
'Golden Splendour', etc.	6–8	(bulb)
Nicotiana affinis	6–10	a
Phlox	7–9	p

Herbaceous plants for a sunny border – a basic list

PLANT NAME	MONTHS	TYPE
FRONT ROW		
Alchemilla mollis	6–7	p
Cerastium tomentosum	6–7	p
Dwarf nasturtium 'Alaska',		
'Empress of India', etc.	6–10	a
Geranium 'Wargrave Pink',		
'Johnson's Blue', 'Striatum'	5–9	p
Heuchera 'Palace Purple',		
'Pewter Moon', etc.	6–8	p
Iberis sempervirens	5–6	(shrub)
Iris pallida variegata	5–6	p
Myosotis (forget-me-not)	5–7	b
Nepeta mussinii (catmint)	5–9	p
Petunia, Alyssum, Pansy	6–10	a
Saxifraga (e.g. 'London Pride')	5–7	p
Sisyrinchium striatum		
(e.g. variegatum)	6–8	p
Stachys lanata	6–7	p
SECOND ROW		
Achillea (e.g. 'Anthea')	6–9	p
Antirrhinum (snap dragon)	6–10	a/b
Astrantia major 'Sunningdale		
Gold', 'Rubra', etc.	6–9	p
Campanula persicifolia	6–9	p
Delphinium belladonna	6–8	p
Gaillardia	7–10	p
Geranium wallichianum		
'Buxton blue'	7–10	p

PLANT NAME	MONTHS	TYPE
Geum	6–7	p
Golden feverfew	5–8	p
Knautia macedonica	6–9	p
Lupin	6–7	
Monarda (bergamot)	7–9	p
Perovskia	7–9	(shrub)
Rudbeckia 'Goldsturm'	8–10	p
Salvia 'East Friesland'	6–8	p
Verbascum	7–8	b/p
THIRD ROW		
Bronze fennel	6–10	p
Campanula lactiflora	6–9	p
Chrysanthemum maximum	7–8	p
Cosmos	7–10	a
Delphinium	6–7/9	p
Geranium 'Claridge Druce',		
'Psilostemon', 'Palmatum'	6–9	p
Helenium autumnale	8–10	p
Hollyhock	7–8	b/p
Lychnis coronaria 'Alba'	6–9	b/p
Malva moschata 'Alba'	7–8	p
Nicotiana affinis	7–10	a/b
Papaver orientale	6–7	p
Phlox paniculata	7–10	p
Thalictrum	6–8	p

NB: It is safer to treat bulbs (tulips, lilies) as annuals in a packed mixed border. They tend to 'disappear'.

Some ground cover plants for shade

Lamium ('White Nancy' or 'Beacon Silver'), Tolmeia menziesi, Geranium macrorhizzum, Bergenia cordifolia, variegated ivies, Saxifraga urbina, Tiarella cordifolia, Tellima grandiflora 'Purpurea', hellebores, epimedium, Arum italicum pictum. For summer try hostas and dicentras, but watch out for slugs.

index